EMILY DICKINSON AND THE MODERN CONSCIOUSNESS

Emily Dickinson and the Modern Consciousness

A Poet of our Time

Kenneth Stocks

St. Martin's Press   New York

First published in the United States of America in 1988

Printed in Hong Kong

ISBN 0–312–00045–6

Library of Congress Cataloging-in-Publication Data
Stocks, Kenneth.
Emily Dickinson and the modern consciousness.
Bibliography: p.
Includes index.
1. Dickinson, Emily, 1830–1886 – Criticism and
interpretation.   I. Title.
PS1541.Z5S86   1988   811'.4   86–6570
ISBN 0–312–00045–6

Contents

Acknowledgements

The author and publishers wish to thank the following who have kindly given permission for the use of copyright material:

Harvard University Press and the Trustees of Amherst College, for the extracts from *The Poems of Emily Dickinson*, edited by Thomas H. Johnson (Cambridge, Mass.: The Belknap Press of Harvard University Press), copyright 1951, © 1955, 1979, 1983 by the President and Fellows of Harvard College.

Little, Brown and Co., for the extracts from *The Complete Poems of Emily Dickinson*, edited by Thomas H. Johnson, copyright 1914, 1929, 1935, 1942 by Martha Dickinson Bianchi; copyright © renewed 1957 by Mary L. Hampson.

Introduction

I have tried in these pages to look at Emily Dickinson's poetry from a viewpoint and in a context which will, I hope, shed new light on her poetry and reveal her more clearly in what I believe to be her true stature and significance as a representative poet in the mainstream tradition of modern Western literature. Here are two quotations which, indicating as they do something of what is involved in being a representative modern poet, should help to make this rather vague statement more explicit.

First, this from Joseph Wood Krutch's book *The Modern Temper*, first published in 1930:

> It is not a changed world but a new one in which man must henceforth live if he lives at all, for all his premises have been destroyed and he must proceed to new conclusions. The values which he thought established have been swept away along with the rules by which he thought they might be attained.
>
> To this fact many are not yet awake, but our novels, our poems, and our pictures are enough to reveal that a generation aware of its predicament is at hand. It has awakened to the fact that both the ends which its fathers proposed to themselves and the emotions from which they drew their strength seem irrelevant and remote.[1]

My second quotation, written nearly fifty years later, points vividly to the same, still unresolved, modern 'predicament' (the writer, Theodore Roszak, is noting the inadequacy of even such great figures of the past as Aristotle, Thomas Aquinas and Dante as present-day guides):

> It does no good at all to quote them at length, to celebrate their insight, to adulate their wisdom. Of course, they are wise and fine and noble, but they stand on the other side of the abyss. They have not, with Conrad's Mr Kurtz, looked into the heart of darkness and seen 'the horror'. No, not even Dante, who travelled all the circles of hell, but always knowing there was a way down and out and through.[2]

It is in relation to these two quotations that we can begin to place Emily Dickinson in her representative role in the mainstream tradition of our poetry. For although in many of her poems she dwelt 'on the other side of the abyss', in many others, and these among her best and most characteristic work, she belongs incontestably to our side. She was no stranger to 'the abyss' or 'the heart of darkness'; the very language of Theodore Roszak in this passage would have been familiar to her, and 'anticipatory echoes' of it can be found in her own work (if the term 'anticipatory echo' is a justifiable one). The first quotation claimed in 1930 that 'a generation aware of its predicament is at hand'; but Emily Dickinson showed in poetry her awareness of it some sixty or seventy years earlier – in advance, even, of the pioneering literature that began to emerge in the concluding decades of the nineteenth century. She was, I believe, the first poet in our language in whom this specifically modern consciousness became fully and lucidly conscious and articulate in poetry, not just in the occasional isolated flash of insight, but in a coherent way that could provide the basis for a continuing exploration of the 'predicament'. This is the Emily Dickinson on whom I have sought particularly to focus attention in these pages. It is only one side of her work, but is, I think, the most crucial and centrally significant side, that in which she most truly reveals herself as a major poet.

'Abyss', 'horror' and 'heart of darkness' are emotive terms which, or the equivalents of which, Emily Dickinson also uses. They express a subjective response – one of a number of possible responses – to a specific modern situation without necessarily revealing the reality of the situation itself. It is thus necessary to distinguish clearly, not only between situation and response, but between the situation as it really is and the form or forms in which it presents itself to the consciousness, and to question whether or how far the one is in conformity with the other. These distinctions are certainly necessary for the understanding of Emily Dickinson, who sometimes in the course of her poetry not only confronted the situation nakedly and direct, but sought also to explore, understand and master it; and explored also a number of responses which are of particular relevance to trends in our own century.

A further point should be mentioned here. The two quotations included above, taken in isolation, seem to suggest a complete break between 'the other side of the abyss' and our side; though this, of course, is not the real intention of the writers. Theodore Roszak goes on to say:

Similarly, it is naïve to summon us to self-knowledge without acknowledging that the deepest self-knowledge of our time begins in the experiencing of radical absurdity and cosmic abandonment. Self-knowledge for us must go through Nietzsche, Kafka, Sartre, Beckett, not around them.

If we are to use fruitfully the resources of the past, we must acquire the power to do so by facing up to and coping with present reality, not take the easy course of skirting round it. Essentially it is a question of the relationship of the perennial in the human situation and experience, as embodied in the living cultural tradition, to what is specifically new in our modern situation. The use of the term 'perennial' (in contrast to what is perishable in men's responses) should help to make the relationship clear. The perennial is not cancelled out by the new, but must be integrated into it at new levels if our responses to present reality are not to provide simply fresh examples of the perishable. In Chapter 1 I have tried to look more closely at this question of the perennial and its continued validity in the changed contexts of our time, with particular reference to Emily Dickinson's poetry, where I think it can be fruitfully studied and exemplified.

Mention should be made of the term 'modern' as I use it, for example, in my title. The term is a notoriously loose one whose scope must be clearly delimited if it is to be used satisfactorily. I think, however, that in relation to the quotations from Joseph Wood Krutch and Theodore Roszak the term as used here defines itself – the 'moderns' are those who dwell on our side of, and have felt and responded in one way or another to, what Roszak calls the 'abyss'. In this sense of the term, Emily Dickinson in a major part of her work is a 'modern'. This does not, of course, make her a 'modernist' poet in any strict meaning of the latter term; in so far as she was a precursor of the 'modernist' movement that began to assert itself shortly after her death, it is only in the sense that she explored in her own way the basic situation that I think can be seen to underlie the authentic manifestations of 'modernism' in their multiplicity of forms, preoccupations and fashions – she can help to clarify our understanding of the 'modernists', though she was not of them. However, in these pages I have concentrated mainly on Emily Dickinson and the basic situation itself, in an effort to understand both a little better.

I have tried to pursue the argument as concretely as possible, relating it at all times to her poetry. For this reason I have had to include a considerable number of her poems in full – the poems themselves are there not only to illustrate, but to prove the validity or otherwise of the points made. I hope this presence of the poems in the text will in itself add an attraction to the volume.

The reference numbers in parentheses at the end of Dickinson's poems are the numbers of the poems in *The Complete Poems of Emily Dickinson*, edited by Thomas H. Johnson (London: Faber and Faber, 1970).

NOTES

1. Joseph Wood Krutch, *The Modern Temper* (London: Jonathan Cape, 1930) pp. 23–4.
2. From a book review by Theodore Roszak, quoted in the periodical *Tract* edited by Peter Abbs.

1

First Approach

I

Emily Dickinson's qualities as a lyric poet, and as perhaps the greatest of women poets, have been widely recognised. Less clearly recognised, I think, is the centrally representative character of her achievement at its best – representative, that is, not of the prevailing fashions of her day, but of its real underlying currents; and centrally so because these currents can be recognised today as the true mainstream currents of Western literature in the period from her death in 1886 up to and including (with certain restrictions) the present. This does not mean that she is representative of the changing forms and preoccupations of the literature of the new age; but, rather, of their underlying consciousness – she is, above all, the poet of the consciousness of the new age. If the new literature can be seen as a consequence, or as a fragmented host of consequences, of a new consciousness that was emerging in the Western world and reaching crisis-point towards the dawn of our century, she explored and brought to conscious expression the consciousness itself; and at her best she did so with an inclusiveness and a directness and intensity of awareness combined with an understanding and control that make a study of her verse in this context particularly illuminating. (Her younger contemporary, Gerard Manley Hopkins, has the intensity and the understanding and control, but not, I think, the inclusiveness. As a committed Catholic in a world of crumbling traditional faiths and values, he lacks the fully representative quality of Emily Dickinson – 'to the blast Tarpeian-fast' was precisely what Emily Dickinson and her world were not, though on his rock he too endured and in his own terms registered the blast.) If I am right in regarding Emily Dickinson as centrally representative in this sense, then a study of her verse should also be a study of the real underlying consciousness (not the consciously held ordinary social consciousness) of the age. These are claims that I hope to justify in the course of this study; more precisely, I hope to provide a context in which she shall speak for herself and, in so doing, speak also for the age.

I want to look a little further at the comparison with Hopkins. Emily

Dickinson says in one of her poems:

> I probed Retrieveless things
> My Duplicate – to borrow –
> A Haggard Comfort springs
>
> From the belief that Somewhere –
> Within the Clutch of Thought –
> There dwells one other Creature
> Of Heavenly Love – forgot –
>   (no. 532)

I don't know whether she would have accepted as her 'Duplicate' in this sense the Hopkins of the so-called 'terrible sonnets', the Hopkins who wrote:

>   Only what word
> Wisest my heart breeds dark heaven's baffling ban
> Bars or hell's spell thwarts. This to hoard unheard,
> Heard unheeded, leaves me a lonely began.
>   ('To Seem the Stranger Lies my Lot')

Emily Dickinson and Hopkins both explored memorably the experience of the reduction of the human to what Hopkins called 'a lonely began', with its accompanying desolations, in a seemingly indifferent universe – 'dark heaven's baffling ban' – 'Of Heavenly Love – forgot – '. Yet there are differences between their explorations beyond what these two quotations indicate. For while the experience is a specifically modern one, arising in its special acuteness from new particular objective causes, it is also, in a wider sense, an age-old phenomenon – a perennial and apparently necessary concomitant of human relationships with natural or divine order. To express it very simply in familiar traditional story terms, Adam experienced it on his expulsion from the Garden, and bequeathed it to all his successors; and it has continued to spread its desolations even in the heart of Christianity – even, for example, in the Christian beginnings, in the 'why hast thou forsaken me?', the words on the Cross. Hopkins' exploration of the experience was in, and remained in, the traditional Christian modes. If he was ultimately secure in his faith, the stress must be on the word 'ultimately'; the security and certainty were hard won, as perhaps they always must be in the deepest and maturest Christian experience. 'I wretch lay wrestling with (my God!) my God'. But while

Hopkins in true Christian fashion wrestled with his God, Emily Dickinson, although she too explored into the traditional, in her deepest and most memorable insights directly confronted and explored the predicament in its changed and more intractable modern form under the pressures of the new scientific—economic—technological order that had not only subordinated real human value to its own necessities but, in her own words, had left

> The Heavens stripped —
> Eternity's vast pocket, picked —
> (no. 587)

In these poems she was the pioneering poet of the new consciousness that was stealing over the later nineteenth century and inherited by our century in various complexities of response. (In one of her poems she has a phrase, 'mortal numeral', that well expresses the reduction of the human to the merely quantitative and statistical — it is a phrase that can be set beside Hopkins' 'lonely began'.) If they started at the same point, he explored into the traditional, she not only into the traditional but into new territory. Yet it is true that they were not only contemporaries, but in a sense 'Duplicates'; and they both watered at the true mainstream currents of the age; though neither knew of, or read, the other.

II

A question might arise as to how, from her small New England base in what was still very much an outer province of Western culture, Emily Dickinson could become a representative poet of the Western mainstream such as I have claimed; and it is a question that should be faced, even though as formulated it derives to some extent from a misunderstanding of the nature of poetry and the poetic imagination.

Goethe once said to Eckermann 'that knowledge of the world is inborn with the genuine poet, and that he needs not much experience or varied observation to represent it adequately'. Eckermann sought an elucidation of this statement. If Goethe maintains that the world is inborn with the poet, he 'of course means only the interior world, not the empirical world of appearances and conventions'. 'Certainly', replied Goethe:

the region of love, hate, hope, despair, or by whatever other means you may call the moods and passions of the soul, is innate with the poet, and he succeeds in representing it. But it is not born with him to know by instinct how courts are held, or how a parliament or a coronation is managed; and if he will not offend against truth while treating such subjects, he must have recourse to experience or tradition . . . yet, had I not the world already in my soul through anticipation, I should have remained blind with seeing eyes, and all experience and observation would have been unproductive labour. The light is there, and the colours surround us; but, if we had no light and no colours in our own eyes, we should not perceive the outward phenomena.[1]

The crucial point is that poetry operates primarily at levels of reality which underlie, but are not apparent in, our ordinary contingent world of everyday conventional experience. No amount of ordinary experience or observation of the everyday world, unassisted by the guiding consciousness of which Goethe speaks, could lead us to these levels. The poet is not unique in possessing this consciousness − it is our common human possession, our underlying awareness, usually vague and unformulated, of our real human needs and values and relationships which are usually obscured or violated in ordinary life. If the poet is unique, it is in his power to intensify the awareness, and to formulate and articulate it in varying modes and under varying pressures, and with its aid to assess and take the measure of his world. This consciousness-guided assessment of the world can go far beyond the reaches of his own immediate experience and observation.

> I never saw a Moor −
> I never saw the Sea −
> Yet know I how the Heather looks
> And what a Billow be.
>
> (no. 1052)

Emily Dickinson, who wrote this, in a number of poems drew her imagery from seafaring and the sea; and this was only one of many such sources which she found in the wider world both of nature and of man. Beyond the reaches of personal experience and observation, social experience must take over − it is our human birthright that it should. What is essential always is the guiding consciousness, the truly seeing eyes without which 'all experience and observation' (social as well as personal) 'would have been unproductive labour'.

Here, for example, is Emily Dickinson herself on this theme of the essential role of the inner, of the guiding consciousness, of, in her own phrase, the 'Central Mood':

> The Outer – from the Inner
> Derives its Magnitude –
> 'Tis Duke, or Dwarf, according
> As is the Central Mood –
>
> The fine – unvarying Axis
> That regulates the Wheel –
> Though Spokes – spin – more conspicuous
> And fling a dust – the while.
>
> The Inner – paints the Outer –
> The Brush without the Hand –
> Its Picture publishes – precise –
> As is the inner Brand –
>
> On fine – Arterial Canvas –
> A Cheek – perchance a Brow –
> The Star's whole Secret – in the Lake –
> Eyes were not meant to know.
>
> (no.451)

This poem is, I think, very characteristic of Emily Dickinson in the way it explores and develops the theme imaginatively in lines densely packed with metaphor. Notice how the second stanza, with its contrasting of the 'Axis' and the 'Spokes', builds on the theme as stated in the first two lines of the poem. The third and fourth stanzas, culminating in the image for the inner light shining in the eyes ('The Star's whole Secret – in the Lake – '), work as a good portrait painting might to make visible the inner reality in the outer appearance, the metaphor performing the role that brush strokes and colour might in the painter's art. Metaphor as she uses it is not mere ornamentation, but is structural in the poem and, despite its abundance, employed with the precision and economy that the structural demands.

Here is another of her poems on the theme of the inner and the outer, but in this case involving the relationship of the human subject to external nature:

> To hear an Oriole sing
> May be a common thing —
> Or only a divine.
>
> It is not of the Bird
> Who sings the same, unheard,
> As unto Crowd —
>
> The Fashion of the Ear
> Attireth that it hear
> In Dun, or fair —
>
> So whether it be Rune,
> Or whether it be none
> Is of within.
>
> The 'Tune is in the Tree — '
> The Skeptic — showeth me —
> 'No Sir! In Thee!'
>
> (no. 526)

Goethe and Emily Dickinson appear to be at one, as all true poets must, on this issue. It is, surely, a first principle in the critical study of poetry that we should look for the inner resource and its implications underlying the poetry. It is too easy, especially in judging contemporary work, to be so dazzled by the conspicuous spinning of the spokes, and blinded by the dust-clouds, that we fail to question whether the poet's inner resources are adequate to his task. This is why the perishable can so often enjoy an immediate fahsionable success; and the imperishable, with its quiet regulation by 'The fine — unvarying Axis', be missed. And even when the imperishable is recognised as such, it is still easy to overlook the underlying inner resource that 'regulates the Wheel'.

My own central task here will be to study the 'Central Mood' underlying and implicit or expressed in Emily Dickinson's poetry; and to show that it is also the 'Central Mood' of the age, to the elucidation of which her poetry can be a guide and lantern. And since the lantern in use must be well alight, I hope the poetry itself will be seen the more clearly for this treatment.

Nevertheless it remains true that immediate experience and observation, with the aid of the inwardly instructed eye that can discern the significant detail and the representative from the trivial mass of data, is a primary and all-important necessity for the poet. Thus, in her poem, 'There's a certain Slant of light', the slant winter light and how it falls had to be experienced and observed. For the rest, the poem dwells within the inner world of meanings and relationships which Goethe knew to be the prior realm of the true poet.

> There's a certain Slant of light,
> Winter Afternoons —
> That oppresses, like the Heft
> Of Cathedral Tunes —
>
> Heavenly Hurt, it gives us —
> We can find no scar,
> But internal difference,
> Where the Meanings, are —
>
> None may teach it — Any —
> 'Tis the Seal Despair —
> An imperial affliction
> Sent us of the Air —
>
> When it comes, the Landscape listens —
> Shadows — hold their breath —
> When it goes, 'tis like the Distance
> On the look of Death —
>
> (no. 258)

I have given this well-known poem in full not only to illustrate the point made above, but for another reason. I have spoken of Emily Dickinson as the poet of a new consciousness which was stealing over the Western world in the late nineteenth century and would soon be working a ferment of change, in a complex diversity of forms and movements, in the arts and literature of the new age. Consider now this poem: the slant winter light falling across the landscape, and the poet's response to it. The deeper meanings (beyond the familiar experience of a change in feeling-tone accompanying a seasonal change of light) are carried in the complexities and depths of the subjective response and their embodiment in the language and structure of the poem.

> Heavenly Hurt, it gives us —
> We can find no scar,

But internal difference,
Where the Meanings, are –

However personal may be this poem, surely this is what the new consciousness did to the literature and arts of the new age, of the decades immediately following Emily Dickinson's death? Even at her most personal she can be most centrally representative.

Consider now this further poem of the changing light, in this case the early spring light:

A Light exists in Spring
Not present on the Year
At any other period –
When March is scarcely here

A Color stands abroad
On Solitary Fields
That Science cannot overtake
But Human Nature feels.

It waits upon the Lawn,
It shows the furthest Tree
Upon the furthest Slope you know
It almost speaks to you.

Then as Horizons step
Or Noons report away
Without the Formula of sound
It passes and we stay –

A quality of loss
Affecting our Content
As Trade had suddenly encroached
Upon a Sacrament.
                              (no. 812)

This poem really only comes into its own with the going of the light, in the last two stanzas. It is the going of the light that gives the 'Heavenly Hurt', felt here explicitly as like the encroachment of 'Trade' upon a 'Sacrament'.

III

It must not be forgotten that the inner world of the poet, or the consciousness which he brings to his work, however particular to himself and to the age in which he lives, is not at bottom peculiar to himself, but is our common human possession, our underlying awareness of human values and relationships that have been lost in ordinary life. This basic common awareness has been an ineradicable element in our whole central tradition of poetry, its necessary substratum or ground, whether or not it finds direct expression in the verse; and it remains so even for a modern consciousness, if that consciousness is not to be at bottom perverse and superficial. As a first approach to Emily Dickinson's verse, before considering more closely the more specific mouldings of her conscious-ness and its modes of expression touched on briefly above, I want to try to show, with the help of a few simple examples, how a primary directness and innocence of perception and response, which is characteristic of her even in more complex work, can lead her straight to this central substratum of experience, and refresh or renew the experience.

Consider, for example, this short lyric:

> Let me not mar that perfect Dream
> By an Auroral stain
> But so adjust my daily Night
> That it will come again.
>
> Not when we know, the Power accosts —
> The Garment of Surprise
> Was all our timid Mother wore
> At Home — in Paradise.
>   (no. 1335)

The poem seeks primarily to convey her own experience of the genesis of a poem – the accosting 'Power . . . The Garment of Surprise . . .'. Yet the words and imagery are so presented that the particular experience immediately becomes an instance of central human experience within what I might call the paradisal substratum of our tradition. The poem not merely dwells in this paradisal substratum, it is itself paradisal and re-creates the paradisal experience as a living and recoverable reality in the present through the particular instance it presents – it rescues, as it should, the living exprience from its entombment in tradition and from conventional pulpit formulations and the likes.

Consider now this poem:

> The Dandelion's pallid tube
> Astonishes the Grass,
> And Winter instantly becomes
> An infinite Alas —
>
> The tube uplifts a signal Bud
> And then a shouting Flower —
> The Proclamation of the Suns
> That sepulture is o'er.
>
>   (no.1519)

From a first simple observation and response, this poem also moves in eight short lines to a rich central world of human meaning; and the effect is wrought with the utmost simplicity. Notice how the 'Proclamation' of the 'shouting Flower' becomes the joint 'Proclamation' of the great sun and the little sun of the dandelion flower simply by putting a final 's' on the word 'Sun' — earth echoing and joining in with cosmic 'Proclamation', responding with new stirrings of life

> The Proclamation of the Suns
> That sepulture is o'er.

Winter entombment and rebirth — the death and resurrection themes traditionally associated with spring — enter the poem through the word 'sepulture' and its connotations. Despite its simplicity and brevity, the poem has so much in it and is truly of the human mainstream. In another poem of the coming of spring, Emily Dickinson says:

> And yet, how still the Landscape Stands!
> How nonchalant the Hedge!
> As if the 'Resurrection'
> Were nothing very strange!
>
>   (no. 74)

'Thou canst but be, but that thou well dost', Gerard Manley Hopkins says to nature. Man is nature's tongue; the 'shouting Flower', though remaining true to itself and to its own contexts, shouts with a human voice and with the human dimensions of entombment and resurrection in it. The primal unity of man and nature is recovered and reasserted, but at a new level.

Here is a third poem:

> How happy is the little Stone
> That rambles in the Road alone,
> And doesn't care about Careers
> And Exigencies never fears –
> Whose Coat of elemental Brown
> A passing Universe put on,
> And independent as the Sun
> Associates or glows alone,
> Fulfilling absolute Decree
> In casual simplicity –
>
> (no. 1510)

Here too, with 'casual simplicity' and in a few short lines, the small particular acquires a mainstream universality. At home in its Copernican-–Newtonian universe, the little stone includes but transcends what the Newtonian scheme has to offer. The whole cosmos is in the small particular, and glows there with a light that transcends without violating the cold Newtonian light. Cosmic necessity and the paradisal are made one – an unveiling of the primal real that is implicit even in the mathematical–scientific picture, though it needed a poet's perceptions to reveal it. If the 'two cultures' theory had been propounded in her day, I doubt whether she would have accepted it. Her own poetry provides ample evidence of her scientific awareness, and her ability to fuse the scientific with her poet's vision or to use science instrumentally for her purpose. 'This timid life of Evidence', as she calls it in one poem, has its own value for her, its integrity, even if it fractures faith; yet her vision can deepen into a unity of apprehension such as is expressed, for instance, in these lines:

> The Scientist of Faith
> His research has but just begun –
> Above his synthesis
> The Flora unimpeachable
> To Time's Analysis –

Here is the whole poem in which these lines appear:

> The Lilac is an ancient shrub
> But ancienter than that
> The Firmamental Lilac

> Upon the Hill tonight –
> The Sun subsiding on his Course
> Bequeaths this final Plant
> To Contemplation – not to Touch –
> The Flower of Occident.
> Of one Corolla is the West –
> The Calyx is the Earth –
> The Capsules burnished Seeds the Stars
> The Scientist of Faith
> His research has but just begun –
> Above his synthesis
> The Flora unimpeachable
> To Time's Analysis –
> 'Eye hath not seen' may possibly
> Be current with the Blind
> But let not Revelation
> By theses be detained –
>
>   (no. 1241)

Scientific and philosophical awareness and understanding, and the poet's imaginative vision seeking to make visible what ' "Eye hath not seen" ' are fused together in a unity of apprehension and poetry. 'Revelation', in the context of the poem, is what is revealed in the poet's vision.

IV

I want to try to clarify a little what I mean by the term 'mainstream' as I have been using it. Our poetry tradition since it came of age has had in every period two main centres – what I call its true mainstream centre, and its establishment centre. (I am ignoring here subsidiary nuclei that might emerge and complicate the immediate picture. Another complicating factor is that the establishment centre is often a battlefield for rival claimants to the position – a contest, perhaps, of traditionalists and innovators – but this is how the establishment changes.) In some periods the establishment centre might stand closer to the true mainstream centre than in others, and it will usually have its channels of access to the mainstream, but it is never identical with the latter; for the establishment is essentially a social phenomenon or grouping, whereas the true mainstream flows at a deeper level of awareness. There are obvious advantages for a mainstream poet if he enters the mainstream from the establishment, and with his merits duly certified by the latter; such a poet, if he retains his membership of both, can become a dominating figure of his age. Nevertheless the establishment is not the only way of access to the mainstream; and, in assessing an age's poetry and poets, and where amidst the clamours and shallows and changing reputations of the age the true deep current of its poetry flows, it is always necessary to maintain the distinction between the two centres. It is particularly necessary with Emily Dickinson who, bypassing the prevailing tastes and fashions and without the benefit of an establishment qualification or blessing, in her best work homed unerringly on the true mainstream. It is also very necessary with Shakespeare, whose establishment status seems to have been far from matching his mainstream greatness. How this could be ceases to be a conundrum when we remember that the establishment is essentially a social formation, fed mainly from approved social circles and institutions, educational and other.

Another term that needs some explanation is 'innocence'. The three examples quoted of what I called a primary innocence of perception and response in Emily Dickinson are, I think, genuine poems of innocence, and should help to make the meaning of the term clear. The innocence is in the consciousness which the poet brings to his work as a poet, in the unclouded and unwarped perceptions of and responses to the real. Where the poem is one which penetrates to, and dwells within, the deeper layers of what I have called the common substratum of real value and relationship which underlies the more specific formulations of the poet's consciousness, it is likely to be, if successful, a recognisable poem of innocence. In what might, by contrast, be called a poem of experience, the innocence of perception and response in the poet's assessment and presentation of a perhaps complex and corrupt world will underlie the poem without necessarily being readily apparent in the finished work. (Shakespeare supremely exemplifies this.)

It will be obvious that innocence, as here understood, has nothing whatever in common with naïvety. Innocence, the true innocence, is the innocence of the real. Naïvety, though a form of innocence, is a false innocence, the innocence of illusion. The two must never be confused. Examples of naïvety can be found in Emily Dickinson, as they can in Blake's 'Songs of Innocence'. But Blake too has his true songs of innocence (for example, 'To Mercy, Pity, Peace, and Love . . .'). And just as the innocence is also in a true poem of experience, so there can be much experience and maturity in a true poem of innocence. (It is perhaps significant that, if the dating is correct, the three poems of innocence quoted from Emily Dickinson are not early products but among her later work.) Poems of innocence and poems of experience is really a false antithesis. The real antithesis is between naïvety and experience.

A poem of innocence, as I have described it, will normally reach towards and, if successful, dwell within the traditional mainstream of our poetry, rather than seek the new mainstream currents of the age. What matters is that the poem should refresh or renew the traditional experience, whether or not it also extends and develops it in new ways. Here is a poem by Emily Dickinson on the very familiar theme of evening peace and nightfall, and made new in the retelling without breaching the perennial:

> The Crickets sang
> And set the Sun
> And Workmen finished one by one
> Their Seam the Day upon.
>
> The low Grass loaded with the Dew
> The Twilight stood, as Strangers do
> With Hat in Hand, polite and new
> To stay as if, or go.
>
> A Vastness, as a Neighbor, came,
> A Wisdom, without Face, or Name,
> A Peace, as Hemispheres at Home
> And so the Night became.
>
> (no. 1104)

And here, as a companion piece, is the flight of summer:

> As imperceptibly as Grief
> The Summer lapsed away —
> Too imperceptible at last
> To seem like Perfidy —
> A Quietness distilled
> As Twilight long begun,
> Or Nature spending with herself
> Sequestered Afternoon —
> The Dusk drew earlier in —
> The Morning foreign shone —
> A courteous, yet harrowing Grace,
> As Guest, that would be gone —

And thus, without a Wing
Or service of a Keel
Our Summer made her light escape
Into the Beautiful.

(no. 1540)

There is in both these poems a courteousness of manner (nature's transience, and the pangs of transience, tempered to a guest-like courteousness of departure) which suggests a deep underlying serenity and security, and at the same time a strict maintenance of a human dimension, in the poet's relations with nature. When this relationship is disrupted, nature can take on an alien, menacing aspect which quite destroys such courtesies. When nature's transience is transferred from the diurnal and seasonal to the biological and human, it asserts itself as death; and death, too, she tempered by an exchange of courtesies in her poem

Because I could not stop for Death —
He kindly stopped for me —

(no. 712)

But whether or not a poet actually writes poems of the traditional mainstream, it is, I think, essential that he should have a primary base or ground in the common human substratum of real value and relationship, into whatever new regions of experience he explores; otherwise his vision is likely to become warped or perverse. Because the common substratum is man's ground of being for his becoming, it is perennial in true poetry, even if only as an unexpressed underlying presence. Certainly with Emily Dickinson, since I must try to follow her into territories more specific to the new age, it seemed very necessary first to show this primary ground from which she works, and which provides her not only with sources of fertility and meaning but with an implicit controlling standard in her best work.

Here, now, is another of her poems, one in which a primary innocence is visibly carried into a world of experience and underlies and measures the sense of loss in experience:

Delight is as the flight —
Or in the Ratio of it,
As the Schools would say —
The Rainbow's way —
A Skein

Flung colored, after Rain,
Would suit as bright,
Except that flight
Were Aliment —

'If it would last'
I asked the East,
When that Bent Stripe
Struck up my childish
Firmament —
And I, for glee,
Took Rainbows, as the common way,
And empty Skies
The Eccentricity —

And so with Lives —
And so with Butterflies —
Seen magic — through the fright
That they will cheat the sight —
And Dower latitudes far on —
Some sudden morn —
Our portion — in the fashion —
Done —

(no. 257)

I said earlier that Emily Dickinson combines intensity of awareness
with an unusual understanding. Primarily the understanding is implicit,
and derives from her basic loyalty to the common substratum of human
relationship and value, the primary real that underlies the poems —
understanding is implicitly present in any true perception of the real,
whether or not it also receives explicit conceptual formulation. But
explicit conceptual formulation, fused with the concrete presentation of
the theme, is what we often do find in Emily Dickinson. The first section
of this poem provides a glimpse of this, in its use of the rainbow theme to
present to the understanding a world that substitutes formula or 'Ratio'
for the living reality in which alone is 'Aliment' or nourishment. But, to
the primary innocence, the rainbow appears and is grasped in its
immediacy.

The fusion of abstract thinking with concrete presentation within a
single poem is very characteristic of Emily Dickinson, and is one of her
great strengths. The fusion is sustained by her ability to use the rich

resources of the language in a way that is reminiscent of English poetry before the seventeenth century's 'dissociation of sensibility' which Eliot diagnosed. Take, for example, this poem on the body–spirit relationship – with its concretisation of abstract thinking in the imagery of the poem, it can be compared in some ways to the Metaphysical heritage of the 'before the dissociation' era without, I think, losing in the comparison:

> The spirit lasts – but in what mode –
> Below, the Body speaks,
> But as the Spirit furnishes –
> Apart, it never talks –
> The Music in the Violin
> Does not emerge alone
> But Arm in Arm with Touch, yet Touch
> Alone – is not a Tune –
> The Spirit lurks within the Flesh
> Like Tides within the Sea
> That make the Water live, estranged
> What would the Either be?
> Does that know – now – or does it cease –
> That which to this is done,
> Resuming at a mutual date
> With every future one?
> Instinct pursues the Adamant,
> Exacting this Reply –
> Adversity if it may be, or
> Wild Prosperity,
> The Rumor's Gate was shut so tight
> Before my Mind was sown,
> Not even a Prognostic's Push
> Could make a Dent thereon –
>
> (no. 1576)

In one respect this poem differs profoundly from the early seventeenth-century Metaphysicals – it is built up on a basis of doubt which is clearly given in the last eight lines. In this respect it is a truly modern poem, on our side of the great divide, yet with a recovery from the past of lost strengths. Between the Metaphysicals and her poem lie the Cartesian body–mind dualism and the other dissociations of the age. It is against this background, the wrenching apart of old unities, that her poem should be measured. This is one of Emily Dickinson's late poems, dating from about 1883. She uses the last few lines of the poem, with small variations, in two other poems of the same period. One of these (no. 1584 – 'Expanse cannot be lost') is included later in these pages. In this poem the line 'Before my Mind was sown' becomes 'Before my Beam was sown', surely a better version – the term 'Beam' can relate to a body—mind unity, whereas 'Mind' might imply a dissociation.

I should like two more of her poems to precede what follows in this section. First, this:

> We knew not that we were to live –
> Nor when – we are to die –
> Our ignorance – our cuirass is –
> We wear Mortality
> As lightly as an Option Gown
> Till asked to take it off –
> By his intrusion, God is known –
> It is the same with Life –
>
> (no. 1462)

This poem has something of an aphoristic flavour which is also very characteristic of Emily Dickinson – her speciality is not the worldly-wise neat but superficial aphorism of everyday conventional living, but the aphorism of a deeper perennial reality of human experience. This capacity for aphoristic brevity makes her one of the most quotable poets in our language. If she has not in fact up to now been one of the most quoted, this may be because insufficient time has elapsed for her wealth of candidates for quotation to pass into the currency of the language, as have Shakespeare's.

Secondly, this presentation in miniature of a tragic situation, of the tensions that make for tragedy – after the aphoristic opening, the particularised situation itself:

> Success is counted sweetest
> By those who ne'er succeed.
> To comprehend a nectar
> Requires sorest need.
>
> Not one of all the purple Host
> Who took the Flag today
> Can tell the definition
> So clear of Victory

As he defeated – dying –
On whose forbidden ear
The distint strains of triumph
Burst agonized and clear!
(no. 67)

James Reeves, in the last paragraph of his introduction to his selection of Emily Dickinson's poems (London: William Heinemann, 1959), speaks of 'that balance of intellect and senses which is fundamental to the apprehension of life in poetic terms'. He suggests that possibly she 'learned the secret from Shakespeare, whom she read constantly. At all events this Shakespearean accent, the balance between the abstract quality of Romance words and the concrete actuality of the Saxon, is never far from her poetry at its finest'. But while her diction, her use of the resources of the language, has been often noticed, the meanings embodied in or immanent in the language and inseparable from the latter in any just estimation of the poetry seem to have received less critical attention. This is an imbalance that I want to try to correct a little in these pages. Meanwhile, here is a little song which surely has a true Shakespearean quality – not an imitating of Shakespeare, but a matching in little:

To this World she returned.
But with a tinge of that –
A Compound manner,
As a Sod
Espoused a Violet,
That chiefer to the Skies
Than to Himself, allied,
Dwelt hesitating, half of Dust,
And half of Day, the Bridge.
(no. 830)

V

Emily Dickinson's verse has both the simplicity and (often) the difficulty that are characteristic of true major poetry. In part, in her case, difficulty can arise from the compression of a complex whole into a small compass without sacrificing the complexity, and from her methods of punctuation which nevertheless, I think, should be respected. Essentially, however, the difficulty is in the implications of the poetry, the difficulty of adequately comprehending the full range and depth of the implications – the sort of difficulty that is inherent in the demands that an imaginative exploration of the underlying real makes on the imaginative response of the reader. Emily Dickinson has a poem which I should like to include in this context:

> Must be a Woe –
> A loss or so –
> To bend the eye
> Best Beauty's way –
>
> But – once aslant
> It notes Delight
> As difficult
> As Stalactite
>
> A Common Bliss
> Were had for less –
> The price – is
> Even as the Grace –
>
> Our lord – thought no
> Extravagance
> To pay – a Cross –
> (no. 571)

To glimpse the 'Stalactite', it is sometimes necessary to make a difficult and arduous subterranean journey.

NOTE

1.   *Conversations of Goethe with Eckermann* (1930 Everyman edn, 1930) pp. 47–8.

2

Poetry and Consciousness

Although innocence and experience are not antithetical in poetry, it is still necessary to maintain a distinction between them. In terms of the poet's consciousness, it is the distinction between the common substratum of the human consciousness and the developed mouldings and formulations of the consciousness that make it particular to the individual poet and to the age in which he lives – though there is inevitably some over-simplification in thus allocating to different levels two such interconnected modes.

There is another way of putting it. Gerard Manley Hopkins says to Nature (or Earth) in one of his poems:

> Thou canst but be, but that thou well dost . . .
> . . . .
> And what is Earth's eye, tongue, or heart else, where
> Else, but in dear and dogged man?
>
> ('Ribblesdale')

Similarly, but, surely, more profoundly and with greater precision, Emily Dickinson says of nature in this fine stanza:

> We pass, and she abides.
> We conjugate Her Skill
> While She creates and federates
> Without a syllable.
>
> (no. 811)

(I said, more profoundly and with greater precision, for Emily Dickinson here goes far beyond Hopkins in recognising that nature is not just 'Thou canst but be', but is 'great creating nature'; and, further, that nature's creating process is a 'federating' process. By 'federating' she means that natural phenomena emerge out of totalities of interconnected and structured complexes – a process that has been more clearly understood, by science as well as philosophically, in our own century than it was in

25

hers. The abstracting mind tends to isolate from their real contexts the phenomena thrown up by the natural process, imposing on nature a falsifying cloak, conventional or of the 'Schools', of our own making – the human mind as the stereotyper of, or the lawgiver to, nature. The term 'conjugate' in the second line of the stanza is very aptly chosen to counteract this falsifying tendency. To conjugate is not simply to express in grammatical language; it is to yoke together, to fuse – note the related terms, conjugal, conjunction. To conjugate is to give expression in sympathetic unity with and responsiveness to nature – what I called earlier the innocence of the real – it is the very opposite of imposing on nature the reifying patterns of our ordinary consciousness and of the 'Schools'.)

However, both quotations are in accord in indicating that it is through man as nature's tongue, eye, heart (primarily, perhaps, man as poet) that nature, all nature including man, becomes articulate and conscious of itself. (Thus the dandelion flower becomes a 'shouting flower', and the little stone testifies to 'absolute decree'.) The innocence, in a poetry that fulfils this function, is in the immediacy and directness of the poem's perception and expression of the underlying unity of man with man and nature; in the recovery, in a successful poem, of the lost unity.

But Hopkins also says, in another poem:

> Manshape, that shone
> Sheer off, disseveral.

Similarly, when Emily Dickinson says, for example,

> Auto da Fé – and Judgement –
> Are nothing to the Bee –
> His separation from His Rose –
> To Him – sums Misery –
> (no. 620)

she too is portraying, in and through a particularised situation, man as 'Sheer off, disseveral'. The two poets are not contradicting themselves in these quotations, but recognising in them an abiding reality of man's situation. Man is part of nature, yet more than nature. But 'more than nature' is also a severance from nature. Man is part of nature, and also something apart from nature. Yet between the unity with and the apartness from there is continuity as well as discontinuity. For nature (again including man) is not only being, but potentiality; and it is in and through the realm of human experience, of man as 'disseveral' and beyond nature, that the potential, in man and nature, is striving to realise itself. The true home of poetry is somewhere in the regions of discontinuous continuity between the two poles of unity and apartness. For some poets – for example, Hopkins and Emily Dickinson – where the experience is at or very near the pole of apartness, the discontinuities may have their precipices and abysses both in the confronting consciousness and in the confronted situation (Emily Dickinson speaks in one poem of 'That awful stranger Consciousness' confronting or 'tilling' an 'abyss'), but it is a function of poetry to attempt its own resolutions of the two poles, to re-establish on new levels the broken harmonies. (Consider, for example, Shakespeare's portrayal, in *Macbeth* and elsewhere, of political power struggles as a disordering, not only of society, but of the order of nature and of man's own nature – in other words, as the disruption of a prior harmony of nature, man and society, a harmony which must be re-established.)

Here is a poem by Emily Dickinson that has, I think, some relevance to the above and to what follows in this section:

> You Left me – Sire – two Legacies –
> A Legacy of Love
> A Heavenly Father would suffice
> Had He the offer of –
>
> You Left me Boundaries of Pain –
> Capacious as the Sea –
> Between Eternity and Time –
> Your Consciousness – and Me –
>
> (no. 644)

Who is the 'Sire' to whom the poem is addressed? The first stanza makes it clear that he is not the 'Heavenly Father'; and presumably also not the Son, even in his human aspect. Hardly, again, an individual human lover – the language of the poem is considerably in excess of what would be appropriate for such a recipient. He is, surely, man himself, *Homo sapiens* – more specifically, in the terms of our tradition, the fallen Adam. Both the love and the pain, in the Christian scheme, are written on the Cross, plain for all to read; yet they are the twin legacies of the fall.

In the remainder of this section I want to look more closely at the relation of the poet's consciousness to his poetry; and at what is meant by the specific mouldings and formulations of the general underlying consciousness that make it particular to the individual poet, as well as humanly significant in a developed way, and, if he is to be a representative poet of his age, particular also to the age. In attempting this, it will be convenient to stay with Hopkins for a while – for Hopkins' work illustrates with exceptional concentration and clarity some of the points I wish to make, and provides, I hope, some proof of their validity.

Hopkins' poetry, with its clearly recognisable Catholic Christian background, vividly exemplifies what I take to be a necessary condition of true mainstream seriousness in poetry – that the poet should have a basis or focal point, a ground of real values and meanings and an adherence to these values and meanings, which is outside his art, but which fuses with the art in the making of the poem and dwells in the poem as an immanent presence and background of the poem's exploring language. This, I think, is the normal relation of the poet's underlying awareness, or consciousness, to the poetry itself.

Hopkins also clearly illustrates what is meant by the specific formulations of the consciousness. In his case it was the traditional Catholic Christian formulation. But here, in such a poet as Hopkins, it is necessary to distinguish between underlying reality and the dogmas and doctrines in which the reality is expressed (or perhaps obscured, if doctrine hardens into a purely external formality of adherence). Hopkins adhered faithfully to the orthodoxies of his Church, certainly; but what as a poet he got from this loyalty was not just a set of dogmas and beliefs but, through these, an intense awareness of and insight into the perennial questions of life's essential values and relationships which are clouded over, falsified and violated in our actual social life ('All is seared with trade; bleared, smeared with toil' ['God's Grandeur']).

This obscuring and falsifying of the person and his human relationships is characteristic, not only of our society's practice, but of its consciousness of itself: for example, in the normal refusal or inability not only of such channels of social awareness as press, radio, television, political and economic and sociological studies and so on but, it must be said, of the great majority of our intellectual representatives of the age, to consider any but contingent truths. This is what I might call the contingent social consciousness, false even where it is true. A true mainstream poetry will penetrate this consciousness, and lay bare the underlying reality – as, for example, Shakespeare in *Timon of Athens* laid bare a society which substituted money for human values and relationships; or, as in this poem by Emily Dickenson (a poem which, in its small but complex compass, penetrates remarkably to the reality of human alienation or 'limiting', to the reduction by society of the person to a mathematical unit or 'mortal numeral'):

Bound – a trouble –
And lives can bear it!
Limit – how deep a bleeding go!
So – many – drops – of vital scarlet –
Deal with the soul
As with Algebra!

Tell it the Ages – to a cypher –
And it will ache – contented – on –
Sing – at its pain – as any Workman –
Notching the fall of the Even Sun!
                              (no. 269)

The distinction made in the previous paragraph, between the doctrines and beliefs and the reality expressed in them, is a vital one for poetry. The poet's approach to life, or world view or vision, however consciously formulated in its upper reaches, essentially lies below the threshold of ideology or dogma in the realm of discernments and values which in Hopkins' case was coherently organised and signposted by his commitment to his religion in its basic concerns and which so unmistakably underlies and informs his poetry. For here again Hopkins illustrates a vital point – it was not a vague general awareness, just as it was not an ideological or dogmatic fixity, but a coherently organised awareness of and living responsiveness to underlying reality that he brought to his poetry. Some degree, at least, of this coherence of meaning and value – or, in an age such as ours, an effort at reordering out of current disorder – is necessary if the poet's awareness is to become a distinctive approach to life that can exercise its potency in the poetry it underlies.

Hopkins chose to establish himself within a traditional system of beliefs. But I have tried to distinguish the achieved attitude from the doctrines and beliefs that in his case mediated it and provided a framework for the coherent organisation of his awareness. It is the ordered awareness, its truths, its values, its discernments, that are the essential; the doctrines and beliefs only one means among a possible many. Certainly an adherence to some discerned basic truth seems essential to the poet of true mainstream seriousness, whether he finds it in old faiths and values, or in the wreckage of these, or in some new contexts of our own age. Shakespeare provides us with an example that differs from Hopkins' in its absence of any explicit apparatus of doctrines and beliefs; and yet with the guiding and transforming presence, especially in the later plays, of an intensely felt and realised underlying vision which expresses itself not usually transcendentally but in the contexts of nature, human action and historic change, and in terms of which he not only takes the measure of his world but points towards some redeeming way.

Hopkins, however great the stresses to which he was subjected, ultimately felt completely secure in his faith. Emily Dickinson, who also established herself primarily within a traditional system of beliefs, was unable to find in it this degree of security. The system was being increasingly riven and undermined and, indeed, already beginning to assume something of a wreckage of old faiths and values; and she had to find her own way in it, still with some of the old signpostings to help her, but without the sure guidance that Hopkins enjoyed. And, in this, Emily Dickinson was representative of her age in a way in which Hopkins was not.

Consider now this poem of hers:

> We learned the Whole of Love —
> The Alphabet — the Words —
> A Chapter — then the mighty Book —
> Then — Revelation closed —
>
> But in Each Other's eyes
> An Ignorance beheld —
> Diviner than the Childhood's —
> And each to each, a Child —
>
> Attempted to expound
> What Neither — understood —
> Alas, that Wisdom is so large —
> And Truth — so manifold!
>
> (no. 568)

Here, in this little poem, is a glimpse of the poet closing the Book of Revelation on which she was nurtured, and standing on the edge of new modes of awareness, new ways of seeking 'Truth', and recognising 'Ignorance' instead of 'Revelation' as her starting point. But although the poem dramatises the situation, it must not be thought that there was in her actual development any such dramatic break between belief and new ways of seeking. We cannot divide her work as a poet into periods and say, for example, that a first period of belief was followed by a period of disbelief and this in turn followed by, say, a period of restructuring traditional belief into consistency or acceptability with new ways and standards of truth-seeking, and so on. It is doubtful whether such division is as useful as is sometimes claimed with any major poet once he is past his juvenilia stage and has reached a degree of maturity; with Emily Dickinson it is quite impossible, and would do great violence to her work. The growth and development of her consciousness was far deeper and more complex than any such schematic imposition could cope with. The old traditional beliefs, or fragments from their wreckage, continued to cling about her and haunt her and assert their meanings throughout her working life as a poet; and poems of belief, or with salvaged splinters of old belief, or poems which do seek to integrate traditional belief into new modes of awareness, continue to coexist side by side with others of a contrary tendency. The point is that, not only for her but for the age, the emergence from the old of a new consciousness was not a simple transition but a traumatic experience, with an accompanying sense of desolation and emptiness and a looking back to the old, or to its wreckage, for lost values that could be reasserted in and through or against the new. What is crucial is the penetration, the depth of insight, that the poet brings to the making of the poem. Some poems, where the deeper inspiration is lacking, might remain imprisoned in a convention of consciously held beliefs; others, where the authentic poet at his true stature takes command, will penetrate to a rich world of real meaning. Consider, for example, how in Yeats's 'The Second Coming' the poet triumphs over the rag-bag of magical beliefs from which he started. Depth of insight, of inspiration, rather than the chronology of the poet's development is what matters most – though, of course, stages of development do have their relevance; more with some poets than with others; less, perhaps, with Emily Dickinson than with most.

This brings us to one characteristic of Emily Dickinson's poetry which could make for some difficulty in adequately getting to grips with her work. To return to the comparison with Hopkins for a moment – one consequence of the latter's clear commitment to Catholicism is that his work has a coherence, an absence of fragmentation of insight, not readily discernible in Emily Dickinson. To contemplate her poetry as a whole is like contemplating a night of abundant stars, each a separate more or less bright pinpoint and with here and there some stars of first and second magnitude shining out among them. Because 'Truth' is 'so manifold', she is constantly seeing new and sometimes contradictory facets of truth, and these particular insights are scattered over a large number of poems – her work is as manifold as truth itself is in her conception. Now the usual type of selection from her work, even though it correctly identifies the best poems or some of them, inevitably reproduces in little the air of fragmentation of the whole from which the poems were taken, in effect presenting them as if they were so many selected anthology pieces. This is what I want to try to avoid. Hopkins' poems clearly have their ground of being in the traditional coherent and well-signposted Catholic Christian order, and his triumph is that in his best work as a poet he makes this traditional order shine forth again as a present reality, as a realm of meaning and value. To recognise this quality in Hopkins, as it so readily can be, is to recognise the nature of the need in coping with Emily Dickinson – the need to facilitate recognition of the consciousness that underlies her poems and is their ground of being, and so to overcome their air of irreducible many-faceted fragmentation.

The problem is that, while Hopkins retained the old signpostings for guidance, Emily Dickinson was exploring without this sure guidance, out in the modern cold, where I must now try to follow her. As Joseph Wood Krutch said in his *The Modern Temper*, all man's 'premises have been destroyed and he must proceed to new conclusions. The values which he thought established have been swept away along with the rules by which he thought they might be attained.' Consider first this poem:

Their Height in Heaven comforts not –
Their Glory – nought to me –
'Twas best imperfect – as it was –
I'm finite – I can't see –

The House of Supposition –
The Glimmering Frontier that
Skirts the Acres of Perhaps –
To Me – shows insecure –

The Wealth I had – contented me –
If 'twas a meaner size –
Then I had counted it until
It pleased my narrow Eyes –

Better than larger values –
That show however true –
This timid life of Evidence
Keeps pleading – 'I don't know.'

(no. 696)

The dashes are perhaps something of a problem in sorting out this poem; particularly the dash after 'I can't see', which combines with its position at the end of the stanza to make a rhythmic or meditative break which the sense must override: 'I can't see the House of Supposition — '. I said a meditative break, for the poem is essentially a meditation on or exploration of the theme of 'This timid life of Evidence', so loudly proclaimed by leading spokesmen of the age but simply meditated on here. We have already noticed these lines from another poem (no. 1241):

> The Scientist of Faith
> His research has but just begun —
> Above his synthesis
> The Flora unimpeachable
> To Time's Analysis —

And the 'Glimmering Frontier' and what lay beyond it was a subject that constantly preoccupied her. Here is another poem:

> This World is not Conclusion.
> A Species stands beyond —
> Invisible, as Music —
> But positive, as Sound —
> It beckons, and it baffles —
> Philosophy — don't know —
> And through a Riddle, at the last —
> Sagacity, must go —
> To guess it, puzzles scholars —
> To gain it, Men have borne
> Contempt of Generations
> And Crucifixion, shown —
> Faith slips — and laughs, and rallies —
> Blushes, if any see —
> Plucks at a twig of Evidence —
> And asks a Vane, the way —
> Much Gesture, from the Pulpit —
> Strong Hallelujahs roll —
> Narcotics cannot still the Tooth
> That nibbles at the soul —
>
> (no. 501)

It is interesting to compare this poem with another poem of similar theme (and, incidentally, of similar metre and the same length) — Vaughan's 'My Soul, there is a Countrie'. Here, for convenience of comparison, is Vaughan's poem:

My Soul, there is a Countrie
Far beyond the stars,
Where stands a winged sentrie
All skilful in the wars,
There above noise, and danger
Sweet peace sits crown'd with smiles,
And one born in a Manger
Commands the Beauteous files,
He is thy gracious friend,
And (O my Soul awake!)
Did in pure love descend
To die here for thy sake;
If thou canst get but thither,
There growes the flowre of peace,
The Rose that cannot wither,
Thy fortresse, and thy ease;
Leave then thy foolish ranges;
For none can thee secure,
But one, who never changes,
Thy God, thy life, thy Cure.

Emily Dickinson says in another poem:

Not Joy, but a Decree
Is Deity —

(no. 1584)

The sort of feeling one can have for such a deity and for His 'Heaven' or 'Tracts of Sheen' (another of her phrases) is far removed from the emotional relationship ('Heart of the heartless world') expressed by Vaughan in his poem. Everything that is in Vaughan's poem has become a broken reed for Emily Dickinson; but the metaphysical question remains, and exerts its fascination. Her mastery of the broken reed and the metaphysics is complete in her poem, in her cool appraisal of the whole range of men's endeavours to penetrate beyond the 'Frontier', from the 'Much Gesture, from the Pulpit' and the 'Strong Hallelujahs' up to and including the metaphysician's own ultimate unresolved dilemma in

And through a Riddle, at the last —
Sagacity, must go —

Here is another of her poems:

> Those — dying then,
> Knew where they went —
> They went to God's Right Hand —
> That Hand is amputated now
> And God cannot be found —
>
> The abdication of Belief
> Makes the Behavior small —
> Better an ignis fatuus
> Than no illume at all —
>
> (no. 1551)

The last two lines of this poem are not a recommendation to grasp at any ignis fatuus that offers itself as a substitute for the pursuit of truth or for genuine belief, but an icy comment on an age which does. She makes her own view abundantly clear in this four-line poem:

> A World made penniless by that departure
> Of minor fabrics begs
> But sustenance is of the spirit
> The Gods but Dregs
>
> (no. 1623)

The 'Gods' who are merely 'Dregs' are the upstart substitute gods who rush in to occupy the vacant seat. We have the situation with us on a considerable and increasing scale today, the cults of the 'minor fabrics', the reversions to astrological and magical practices and beliefs — it is remarkable how a hundred years ago Emily Dickinson saw its coming with such clarity. One thing she could hardly be expected to have foreseen is the role being played today by UFOs and visitants from outer space. A further consequence of the 'abdication of Belief' is the emergence of doctrines of the convenient or useful fiction and their elevation to a sort of philosophic status, the test being: not, is it true? But the pragmatic one, does it work in practice? Emily Dickinson, in one of her poems, has her own precise brief phrase — 'A Fiction superseding Faith'. Here again, in this phrase, she has her finger on the pulse of our time. 'A Fiction superseding Faith' precisely describes what has been a central preoccupation of our century, not only at various levels of crudity in ordinary life, but in its arts and sciences. At its best in the latter it has been a heroic and able attempt, against a background of seeming meaninglessness and cosmic abandonment, to find and assert some specifically human meaning – a fiction because it can find no foothold or sanction in any deeper reality that we can discern, but nevertheless of profound human meaning and value. As for the 'Truth' itself, Emily Dickinson is severely uncompromising in this poem:

> Truth – is as old as God –
> His Twin identity
> And will endure as long as He
> A Co-Eternity –
>
> And perish on the Day
> Himself is borne away
> From Mansion of the Universe
> A lifeless Deity.
>
> (no. 836)

The point is reinforced in this uncompromising stanza from another poem:

> Inherited with Life –
> Belief – but once – can be –
> Annihilate a single clause –
> And Being's – Beggary –
>
> (no. 377)

The age has reduced 'Being' to 'Beggary', man in his true being to 'mortal numeral'. Her recognition of this situation does not, of course, make it a final resting place for her. Sometimes, as we shall see, she does rest in it, confronting the situation direct; and sometimes explores various responses to it; but at times seeking also, with her grasp of the underlying real, to salvage what is perennial and valid from the wreckage of old 'Belief'.

A brief additional note on God, truth and science. An age which has enthroned the scientific method can claim its own integrity in the pursuit of truth whatever the consequences. In her poem 'Their Height in Heaven comforts not' (no. 696), Emily Dickinson explores the 'timid life of Evidence' and its consequences. On the other hand, her poem on truth as God's 'Twin' and 'Co-Eternity' propounds an uncompromisingly Platonist position. The gulf between the two is perhaps not completely unbridgeable. To the extent that science could tolerate or lend substance to the idea of God, a God who would be 'Not Joy, but a Decree', truth too could be granted a reprieve – absolute decree and truth are twins. Science's pathway to the 'God of Decree' lay through its ascertainment of the predictable regularities of the cosmic processes. It is a sort of return to the Platonic forms via a new route. As we shall see later, Emily Dickinson explored this pathway too, and found there a source of strength and reassurance though not the sort of comfort expressed by Vaughan in his 'My Soul, there is a Countrie'. Of course, there is still the epistemological question as to how we can proceed from something that is scientifically valid for us to what it is in itself. Emily Dickinson has her own comment on this in this little epistemological poem:

> Perception of an object costs
> Precise the Object's loss –
> Perception in itself a Gain
> Replying to its Price –
>
> The Object Absolute – is nought –
> Perception sets it fair
> And then upbraids a Perfectness
> That situates so far –
> (no. 1071)

Her 'Lilac' poem (no. 1241), included in chapter 1, is also relevant to this.

I should like to conclude this section with another of her poems. Although it would be an over-simplification to categorise some of her poems as essentially poems that present and appraise a situation, and others as poems of personal and human response to a given situation (an over-simplification because an emotive response can be implicit in the presentation of the situation and is often best left that way), this poem is very much one of personal response:

> Somewhere upon the general Earth
> Itself exist Today –
> The Magic passive but extant
> That consecrated me –
>
> Indifferent Seasons doubtless play
> Where I for right to be –
> Would pay each Atom that I am
> But Immortality –

> Reserving that but just to prove
> Another Date of Thee –
> Oh God of Width, do not for us
> Curtail Eternity!
>
> (no. 1231)

To me this seems a profoundly beautiful little poem – a cry or prayer from out in the modern cold, where the loss of real human values in the order we have conjured up (lost, that is, to us, but perhaps not to the 'general Earth') is compounded by the threatened loss or diminution of the dimension of 'Eternity'. The 'God of Width', the possible curtailer of 'Eternity', is no longer the God with whom Hopkins wrestled or from whom Vaughan drew his comfort, but the God of the new scientific and social order that developed from the decisive seventeenth-century changes, the God who is now, in Emily Dickinson's words, 'Not a Joy, but a Decree'.

3

Manacle, Death, Time

I should like to begin this section with a fairly close look at the following poem by Emily Dickinson (it is, I think, a key poem for the understanding both of herself as poet and of our time — a poem in which the personal, subjective experience embodied in it is very clearly also representative of the consciousness of our age):

> Let Us play Yesterday —
> I — the Girl at school —
> You — and Eternity — the
> Untold Tale —
>
> Easing my famine
> At my Lexicon —
> Logarithm — had I — for Drink —
> 'Twas a dry Wine —
>
> Somewhat different — must be —
> Dreams tint the Sleep —
> Cunning Reds of Morning
> Make the Blind — leap —
>
> Still at the Egg-life —
> Chafing the Shell —
> When you troubled the Ellipse —
> And the Bird fell —
>
> Manacles be dim — they say —
> To the new Free —
> Liberty — Commoner —
> Never could — to me —
>
> 'Twas my last gratitude
> When I slept — at night —

'Twas the first Miracle
Let in – with Light –

Can the Lark resume the Shell –
Easier – for the sky –
Wouldn't Bonds hurt more
Than Yesterday?

Wouldn't Dungeons sorer grate
On the Man – free –
Just long enough to taste –
Then – doomed new –

God of the Manacle
As of the Free –
Take not my Liberty
Away from Me –

(no. 728)

It should help to illumine this poem if we look at it in the light of a key poem of an earlier period – Wordsworth's 'Immortality Ode'. The theme of her poem, in its beginning, has something in common with that of the 'Immortality Ode'; but, in its exploration and development of the theme, as well as in form and scale, it is far removed from Wordsworth's – the consciousness behind it is not only more uncertain and insecure, but is as centrally representative of her time and ours as Wordsworth's was of the Romantic mainstream of his day. The poem's point of departure is significant. It begins, not with the shining of 'angell-infancy' (to quote from an earlier treatment of the theme, Vaughan's 'The Retreate'), nor with Wordsworth's 'visionary gleam', but with the 'famine' and 'dry wine' of a prevailing system that excludes or obscures real human need and value; though intimations of 'somewhat different' haunt the child as they continue to haunt Wordsworth's growing boy even through the 'shades of the prison-house' that are beginning to close around him (notice the tentativeness of the 'somewhat different' compared to Wordsworth's confident naming of the source and meaning of the intimations).

Still at the Egg-life –
Chafing the Shell –
When you troubled the Ellipse –
And the Bird fell –

The child's 'fall' is the crucial event of the poem – the breaking of the primal bonds, the falling into the apartness of a man-made order set over against nature and real human value. Whatever philosophical or theological explanations we give of the experience (basically a subject –object dualism in our understanding and practice, with all that stems from this dualistic approach), the experience itself is universal and perennial in human life, but impinging with a special severity which makes it in some respects qualitatively different in our age. It is at this point that Emily Dickinson's poem departs most radically from Wordsworth's – it is a significant departure of the complex modern consciousness, under the pressures of the age, from the optimism of the Romantic dawn. In Wordsworth's poem, the breaking of the primal bonds, the fading of the 'visionary gleam', is all loss; the consolation is in what can be salvaged from the loss and integrated into the mature experience. In her poem, however, the falling into apartness appears both as social and cosmic 'Manacle' and as a creative leap for freedom. Primarily, in the experience as presented in the poem, the felt 'Manacle' is social – the manmade world of 'Lexicon' and 'Logarithm', utilitarian, attached to the purely quantitative and statistical, imposing its mechanising pattern on nature and the cosmos, the world of 'mortal numeral', of 'Limit – how deep a bleeding go!' God, who 'troubled the Ellipse', is implicated in the child's fall (leap for freedom), and presumably engineered it (God of the 'Free'). As she says in another poem:

> Is Eden's innuendo
> 'If you dare?'
> (no. 1518)

But God is also the God of the 'Manacle', of necessity, God of the celestial and the social mechanics. The poem presents and explores a view of the human situation and a response to it which, from our twentieth-century perspective and using a twentieth-century term, we can recognise as essentially existentialist. Written in or about 1863, the poem is a pioneering one in this mode, reaching beyond her day towards something that has only become familiar in our own century, though behind it is the Kantian picture of individual man with his inner ethical freedom confronting an external iron necessity. Through most of its length the poem is conversational in tone (talking conversationally to God, essentially the poet talking to herself). At the end, however, it modulates into the four-line prayer of the final stanza. Something of the lonely insecurity underlying and experienced in the existentialist response to what is felt as social and cosmic necessity (or 'Manacle') finds expression in this prayer and in the 'Then – doomed new' of the preceding stanza.

To take the contrast with Wordsworth's poem a step further: Wordsworth's poem makes it own reconciliation of primal unity and apartness, its own re-establishment of the broken harmonies with nature and the transcendental, at a new level of mature human awareness. It is the typical, central Romantic reconciliation, expressed in this poem with exceptional felicity and clarity. A modern consciousness, one which had felt and responded to the full impact of the Industrial–Technological–Utilitarian Revolution with all its human deprivations and other consequences, would criticise this Romantic reconciliation as too premature, too easy and inadequate, relying too readily on inherent human goodness and cosmic or divine benevolence, failing to plumb to its full depths the reality of human social and cosmic alienation. Certainly Emily Dickinson, bringing to the situation a consciousness basically Christian but moulded to her age, allowed into her poem no prospect of reconciliation, neither the Romantic one nor the ultimate guilt-conscious Christian one expressed in Dante's words, 'His will is our peace' – only, in this poem, the lonely and insecure existentialist response to continuing and unresolved menace.

Before proceeding, here is another of her poems – a minor one, but interesting as a minor echo of aspects of the previous poem:

> The butterfly obtains
> But little sympathy
> Though favorably mentioned
> In Entomology –
>
> Because he travels freely
> And wears a proper coat
> The circumspect are certain
> That he is dissolute –
>
> Had he the homely scutcheon
> Of modest Industry
> 'Twere fitter certifying
> For Immortality –
>
> (no. 1685)

The focus here is clearly on the social relationship. The free spirit, symbolised by the butterfly, is subjected to society's utilitarian appraisal, and found wanting. The honour of being accorded the favourable attentions of science is a two-edged one in the context of the poem, a classifying and pinning down.

The existentialist type of response to the situation presented in the'Manacle and Freedom' poem at the beginning of this section is representative of only one side of Emily Dickinson, though a significant side for our time. In some of her finest poems the situation itself, in varying versions and forms of expression, is again presented, sometimes with a nightmarish intensity, but without the existentialist solution being either sought or expressed. Situation and response – we can distinguish the two, though they are fused together in the poem. For the remainder of this section I want to focus attention on the basic situation itself; in the next section, to look a little further at the existentialist response; and in later sections to look at other of her responses.

II

To return for a moment to Emily Dickinson's 'Manacle and Freedom' theme: the theme is not only written in the mechanised society with, in Dr F.R. Leavis's words,[1] its 'implicit reduction of human life to mere instrumentality'; it is also written for us in the stars – in the spectacle of our planet earth as a qualitatively emerging, living process, evolutionary and, through man, historical, in a cosmic environment of inexorable necessity, and in the Cartesian–Newtonian reduction of earth itself to that part of earth's heritage which earth shares with the rest of the cosmos. I have already referred to Kant's picture of individual man with his inner ethical freedom confronting an external iron necessity. It can be taken as a picture of modern Western man confronting the world he himself has conjured up. It can also be taken as a picture of qualitative earth confronting the cosmos. There is indeed a remarkable correspondence between the social pattern and the cosmic pattern as unveiled by the Newtonian science. It is as if, instead of collaborating with earth's living, qualitative growth, we were shaping on Earth's surface a sort of replica of the Newtonian cosmic environment, establishing here something like that environment's hostility to life from which, however, earth is shielded in space, but not here, by its protective atmosphere. If it is true, as Hopkins suggests, that the poet is earth's consciousness and tongue, it could be earth itself speaking to man the maker of this surface environment the prayer of the last four lines of the poem:

> God of the Manacle
> As of the Free –

Take not my Liberty
Away from Me –

I want at this point to introduce another and contrasting theme – an old theme, long-established in our tradition, but bearing it in a gift of perennial renewal. At the dawn of our present social order Milton's 'Nativity Ode' celebrated an earlier dawn which introduced a sense of unique historic change with qualitative newness breaking through and investing nature as well as man. (Qualitative newness, when it enters man's consciousness, really does seem also to invest nature, for the nature we experience and know always wears the cloak of our own consciousness. For example, the disordered nature Macbeth experienced was wearing the cloak of his own and his society's disruption; just as the green branches advancing from Birnam Wood were not only military camouflage but, in the play's poetic context, an expression of nature invested in the human expectation of renewed harmony and peace.)

This theme of qualitative newness breaking through, in nature and in her own consciousness, is of course abundantly and richly present in Emily Dickinson's verse. But of the third element in the theme, qualitative historic change, there is little evidence in her work; and in this, too, she was representative of her age.

Milton's 'Nativity Ode' was the last great song in our language of qualitative renewal in history, man and nature, all three in combination (a frequent theme of Shakespeare's) before Christianity (through Puritanism, chiefly) was remodelled to the requirements of the new order and nature put on its Cartesian–Newtonian cloak. The new order, in its triumphant struggle against old obscurantism, despotism, entrenched authority and received doctrine, threw up certain values – they are the familiar liberal values of our society – which transcend their immediate economic and political power base and, abstractly considered, take on a character analogous to natural law which, if valid at all, is valid for all times and places. It was thus possible for Alexander Pope in his day to be the voice of a civilisation which felt that it had emerged from historic struggle into an achieved timelessness. To this day this assumption of timelessness has remained ineradicably in our social consciousness. It is in the attachment of liberal idealism to abstract idea and principle. It is in the Romantic vision of a timeless, eternal nature, a general organic timelessness replacing the abstract general validity of idea and natural law. It is in the attachment of society to the quantitative and statistical; in its readiness to admit change and growth within the system only quantitatively, and even then only within the framework of an assumed immutability. And it is in these lines of Emily Dickinson's:

> Next time, to tarry,
> While the Ages steal –
> Slow tramp the Centuries,
> And the Cycles wheel!

Time for Emily Dickinson is not qualitative historic time, but the timeless time of the mechanised celestial systems and of the social–historic systems conceived as endlessly repetitive like the repetitive production processes of our system, Time as measured mathematically by the clock and calendar. This timeless time is closely linked in her consciousness with death. The death–time linking is very clear in the fine poem from which the four lines quoted above are taken. Here is the poem in full:

> Just lost, when I was saved!
> Just felt the world go by!
> Just girt me for the onset with Eternity,
> When breath blew back,
> And on the other side
> I heard recede the disappointed tide!
>
> Therefore, as One returned, I feel
> Odd secrets of the line to tell!
> Some Sailor, skirting foreign shores –
> Some pale Reporter, from the awful doors
> Before the Seal!
>
> Next time, to stay!
> Next time, the things to see
> By Ear unheard,
> Unscrutinized by Eye –
>
> Next time, to tarry,
> While the Ages steal –
> Slow tramp the Centuries,
> And the Cycles wheel!
>
> (no. 160)

The last stanza provides the temporal and timeless setting for the drama portrayed and envisaged in the poem.

The death–time association is also wonderfully at work in this poem:

> Safe in their Alabaster Chambers –
> Untouched by Morning –
> And untouched by Noon –
> Lie the meek members of the Resurrection –
> Rafter of Satin – and Roof of Stone!
>
> Grand go the Years – in the Crescent – above them –
> Worlds scoop their Arcs –
> And Firmaments – row –
> Diadems – drop – and Doges – surrender –
> Soundless as dots – on a Disc of Snow –
>
> (no. 216)

As for the prospect of plucking the flower of immortality from the death–time process, here is a wryly ironical visualisation of the prospect:

> It is an honorable Thought
> And makes One lift One's Hat
> As One met sudden Gentlefolk
> Upon a daily Street
>
> That We've immortal Place
> Though Pyramids decay
> And Kingdoms, like the Orchard
> Flit Russetly away
>
> (no. 946)

Consider this 'Clock' poem:

> A Clock stopped –
> Not the Mantel's –
> Geneva's farthest skill
> Can't put the puppet bowing –
> That just now dangled still –
>
> An awe came on the Trinket!
> The Figures hunched, with pain –
> Then quivered out of Decimals –
> Into Degreeless Noon –

It will not stir for Doctors —
This Pendulum of snow —
This Shopman importunes it —
While cool — concernless No —

Nods from the Gilded pointers —
Nods from the Seconds slim —
Decades of Arrogance between
The Dial life —
And Him —

(no. 287)

The poem can be read not only at its face value, but as a little parable of
death and time; of man ('the puppet bowing') with his little span, his built-
in obsolescence, tied through the clock-world to the celestial mechanics.
The cosmic scale of the plight of the dangling puppet of the clock-face is
clearly given in these two lines from another of her poems, 'It was not
Death':

When everything that ticked — has stopped —
And Space stares all around —

Here is this poem in full:

It was not Death, for I stood up,
And all the Dead, lie down —
It was not Night, for all the Bells
Put out their Tongues, for Noon.

It was not Frost, for on my Flesh
I felt Siroccos — crawl —
Nor Fire — for just my Marble feet
Could keep a Chancel, cool —

And yet, it tasted, like them all,
The Figures I have seen
Set orderly, for Burial,
Reminded me, of mine —

As if my life were shaven,
And fitted to a frame,

> And could not breathe without a key,
> And 'twas like Midnight, some –
>
> When everything that ticked – has stopped –
> And Space stares all around –
> Or Grisly frosts – first Autumn morns,
> Repeal the Beating Ground –
>
> But, most, like Chaos – Stopless – cool –
> Without a Chance, or Spar –
> Or even a Report of Land –
> To justify – Despair.
>
> (no. 510)

There is not a grain of comfort in this poem, not a gleam of Hopkins'

> Across my foundering deck shone
> A beacon, an eternal beam

or of any other transcendental or human (existentialist or other) response to human need; only an expression, comfortless and total, of the experienced reality of human estrangement.

The words just quoted from Hopkins' poem 'That Nature is a Heraclitean Fire' are preceded by this:

> Manshape, that shone
> Sheer off, disseveral, a star, death blots black out; nor mark
> Is any of him at all so stark
> But vastness blurs and time beats level.

This is Hopkins' version of the human predicament in its estrangement from primal being. Hopkins still clung to the traditional supports of man in his estrangement. For Emily Dickinson and her and our society, these supports were breaking down. Instead of the traditional order, what she saw was wreckage, 'Without a Chance, or Spar'. For both of them, 'time beats level' – the temporal order is stubbornly resistant to true human value, the realm of anonymity ('vastness blurs'), levelling, death that 'blots black out'. Death and time are the twin arbiters of human fate in the absence of the transcendental answer that still signalled to Hopkins.

After this poem of pure confrontation with the situation, I should like to conclude this section with two more of her poems of death–time response.

First, this poem, with its interesting sidelight on time and history:

As far from pity, as complaint –
As cool to speech – as stone –
As numb to Revelation
As if my Trade were Bone –

As far from Time – as History –
As near yourself – Today –
As Children, to the Rainbow's scarf –
Or Sunset's Yellow play

To eyelids in the Sepulchre –
How dumb the Dancer lies –
While Color's Revelations break –
And blaze – the Butterflies!

(no. 496)

At first sight the line 'As far from Time – as History' strikes strangely in this context. Time and history are intimately connected – history is time organised to human ends. The poem, however, is concerned with the unbridgeable distancing, or separation, of the dead from the living; and the line in question only has meaning in the pattern of the poem if this distancing, or separation, similarly occurs between time and history. This, in fact, is precisely what does occur when time is conceived, not as a qualitative historic process, but in the ahistorical way described earlier in this section. Past time (history), where a true historical consciousness is lacking, tends to appear as dead time, fossilised into a sort of timelessness (like the state of the dead in the poem) set over against the hectic time-ridden living of the present and the transient beauties of nature and nature's ephemera. And where the continued presence of the past is felt or sought or observed or conserved in the present, what we tend to get is not a true living and dynamic historical interrelationship of past and present, but a sense of the historic past as a timeless immanence in the present. (This, I think, partly explains both the appeal and the limitation of much of John Betjeman's work.) Emily Dickinson says in another poem

It is the Past's supreme italic
Makes this Present Mean.

(no. 1498)

These lines acutely pinpoint a practice which has become very familiar in some modern poetry, the use of 'the Past's supreme italic' as a foil to a rendering of what is felt as present meanness or squalor – most notably, perhaps, in Eliot (for example, 'Sweeney Among the Nightingales'). Nevertheless, her lines do not adequately account for the phenomenon of 'Present meanness' – an 'italicised Past' does not make the 'Present mean', it merely highlights a meanness or littleness or squalor which is really there and which derives from other causes which are largely specific to, or, where perennial, intensified in our age. Elsewhere in her work she explicitly recognises this, in her recognition of 'mortal numeral', 'Limit – how deep a bleeding go', or as when, for example, she says

> The abdication of Belief
> Makes the Behavior small
> (no. 1551)

But the question of the real living historical interconnection and casual continuity (which can also at times be a discontinuity) of past and present remains; it is not one that normally springs very readily and lucidly to the forefront of a typical modern consciousness of our society, whether expressed in ordinary discourse or in our politics, economic studies, literature or prevailing philosophies.

Finally, this poem:

> The Months have ends – the Years – a knot –
> No power can untie
> To stretch a little further
> A Skein of Misery –
>
> The Earth lays back these tired lives
> In her mysterious Drawers –
> Too tenderly, that any doubt
> An ultimate Repose –
>
> The manner of the Children –
> Who weary of the Day –
> Themself – the noisy Plaything
> They cannot put away –
>
> (no. 423)

Death and time (calendar time, in this instance) are fused together in this poem. Man, 'the noisy Plaything' who, though grown weary, cannot put himself away, is put away by nature's gift to life of built-in obsolescence, measured by the calendar.

NOTE

1.   In his *D. H. Lawrence: Novelist* (London: Chatto & Windus, 1955).

4

The Existentialist Response

Although as an explicit philosophical movement existentialism belongs to the twentieth century, its father-philosophers were Kierkegaard and, as a background presence, Kant, and all the conditions for its emergence as a stance or a way of life or an explicit philosophy already existed in the consciousness of Emily Dickinson's time — her distinction is that she brought to conscious expression in poetry what was potentially already there; and, in doing so, she speaks with a voice more recognisably attuned to our century than to her own. To use her own words, we see her

> better for the Years
> That hunch themselves between —
> The Miner's Lamp — sufficient be —
> To nullify the Mine —
>
> (no. 611)

Rightly understood, she herself, in and through her poetry, can be a 'Miner's Lamp' to help nullify the darkness that still underlies much of our surface attitudes and responses.

What is remarkable in the 'Manacle and Freedom' poem included at the beginning of the previous chapter is the understanding revealed in it of the basic existentialist position, its awareness of the nature of the situation and the nature of the response — not only in its dialectical interplay of 'Manacle' and 'Freedom'; but in its recognition that the subject of the existentialist response is not man in his primal being, but fallen man, man thrust into apartness, to whom in his apartness the natural and social orders assume the character of an external necessity against which the individual, with his sense of inner freedom and value, must assert himself and create his own meanings; and in its expression, in the four-line prayer at the end of the poem, of an accompanying sense of lonely insecurity which can reach extreme forms in the existentialist 'angst'. One essential basic ingredient of existentialism not explicit in this poem is death or, more precisely, the death—time linkage, but this is very amply catered for in other of her poems — the concept of time, that is, in which true history is annulled and death reigns. From being a qualitative flowing, time hangs spatialised from the cosmic mechanics, and history becomes a marked-out, two-dimensional field for individual and probably unsuccessful human exploits. Its God is Emily Dickinson's 'God of Width', the curtailer of eternity.

Emily Dickinson not only confronted and explored in poetry the basic situation, the human predicament as it presented itself to the underlying consciousness of the age, in response to which existentialism as a working philosophy emerged; she also, first among the poets of our language, brought to conscious definition in poetry the emergent existentialist consciousness itself. Here are several poems in which she explores the consciousness both in itself and through some of its ramifications. First, this:

> No Rack can torture me –
> My Soul – at Liberty –
> Behind this mortal Bone
> There knits a bolder One –
>
> You cannot prick with saw –
> Nor pierce with Scimitar –
> Two Bodies – therefore be –
> Bind One – the Other fly –
>
> The Eagle of his Nest
> No easier divest –
> And gain the Sky
> Than mayest Thou –
>
> Except Thyself may be
> Thine Enemy –
> Captivity is Consciousness –
> So's Liberty.

> (no. 384)

'Captivity' and 'Liberty' are both in the consciousness. It is not a return to the old theme of 'stone walls do not a prison make', but a response to a crisis of the human spirit in a new situation; it should be read in the light of the 'Manacle and Freedom' poem. 'Captivity' and 'Liberty', 'Manacle' and 'Freedom', are what Heidegger calls 'inauthentic' and 'authentic' living.

Here is another poem:

> To be alive — is Power —
> Existence — in itself —
> Without a further function —
> Omnipotence — Enough —
>
> To be alive — and Will!
> 'Tis able as a God —
> The Maker — of Ourselves — be what —
> Such being Finitude!
>
> (no. 677)

Man, condemned to finitude in an unresponsive universe, is thrown on his own God-like resources to be the 'Maker' of himself. Though just to be alive (that is, with true aliveness, with something of life's primal freshness still clinging to it — not 'inauthentic' living, in which true aliveness is lost in utilitarian function) in itself is value.

> A Deed knocks first at Thought
> And then — it knocks at Will —
> That is the manufacturing spot
> And Will at Home and well
>
> It then goes out an Act
> Or is entombed so still
> That only to the ear of God
> Its Doom is audible —
>
> (no. 1216)

It is in the translation of 'Thought' into 'Will' into 'Act' that the existentialist authentic is revealed. But here is a dilemma. The making of poetry, true poetry, is surely authentic action of the highest order. But suppose the maker pursues his work in strict privacy, with little hope of or attempt at publication and with the likelihood that it will perish with him when he dies, what then of a lifetime's authenticity of action?

> Only to the ear of God
> Its Doom is audible —

Evidently, for the poetry to qualify as authentic action, it is necessary not only to write it but to get it published or at least circulated or made known to others in some form — action must not only take place, it must be seen to take place, if the inner reality of the person is to be disclosed and verified; and this, formulated in various ways including in the higher abstractions of some leading schools of philosophy, is received doctrine in an age which has not only put out the all-seeing Eye of God but equally distrusts unverified insights of the imagination. To be authentic in existentialist terms, the action need not necessarily be successful; probably it will not be, for the existentialist theme arises from, is a response to, what is felt in present actuality as a confrontation of the free person with external necessity. (For example, Emily Dickinson, on a subject that touched her closely, said:

> Publication – is the Auction
> Of the Mind of Man
> (no. 709)

– the reduction of literature and its values to a market commodity, subject to the necessities of the market. She also says, in the same poem:

> Reduce no Human Spirit
> To Disgrace of Price

– the human spirit arrayed against the drive to reduce it to 'mortal numeral', to a mere instrument or thing. Sometimes, as in this example, the external necessity is felt as essentially socio-economic; but it also, in the consciousness of the age, acquires a cosmic dimension.)

All this leads on to the next poem:

> A Plated Life – diversified
> With Gold and Silver Pain
> To prove the presence of the Ore
> In Particles – 'tis when
>
> A Value struggle – it exist –
> A Power – will proclaim
> Although Annihilation pile
> Whole Chaoses on Him –
> (no. 806)

Here, in these eight lines, is the essence of the basic existentialist situation and response – the 'Plated Life' (the ordinary or inauthentic); the pains of authenticity ('Gold and Silver Pain') with its struggle to assert 'Value' in confrontation with iron necessity; 'Annihilation', the piling on of 'Chaoses'. It is basically a despairing attitude; yet, within its conceptual framework, a noble one, giving to the authentically human a sort of tragic grandeur.

> This Consciousness that is aware
> Of Neighbors and the Sun
> Will be the one aware of Death
> And that itself alone
>
> Is traversing the interval
> Experience between
> And most profound experiment
> Appointed unto Men –
>
> How adequate unto itself
> Its properties shall be
> Itself unto itself and none
> Shall make discovery.
>
> Adventure most unto itself
> The Soul condemned to be –
> Attended by a single Hound
> Its own identity.
>
> (no. 822)

This poem is worth pondering carefully. Its four short stanzas are dense with the properties of an existentialist attitude – the aloneness, the reliance on the self (what in another poem she calls the 'Columnar Self'), the awareness of death as an abiding presence and a crucial event, the hunt for personal identity in a world that reduces personal identities to 'mortal numeral' or swamps them in superficial social relationships.

Consider now this poem:

> More Life – went out – when He went
> Than Ordinary Breath –
> Lit with a finer Phosphor –
> Requiring in the Quench –
>
> A Power of Renowned Cold,
> The Climate of the Grave

A Temperature just adequate
So Anthracite, to live –

For some – an Ampler Zero –
A Frost more needle keen
Is necessary, to reduce
The Ethiop within.

Others – extinguish easier –
A Gnat's minutest Fan
Sufficient to obliterate
A Tract of Citizen –

Whose Peat lift – amply vivid –
Ignores the solemn News
That Popocatapel exists –
Or Etna's Scarlets, Choose –

(no. 422)

Anthracite, more than other fuels, continues burning when it is shut down and the draught excluded. A life of pure 'Anthracite', and 'authentic' life, will continue glowing even in the grave. The existentialist death-theme, the 'authentic' and the 'inauthentic' dying, is presented in this poem, in vivid imagery, more than sixty years before Heidegger.

This brings us to another aspect of existentialism, its expression in action, its legendary heroes and doomed 'authentic' figures of the two-dimensional historic field – for example, Thom Gunn's 'Sad Captains',

all
the past lapping them like a
cloak of chaos.

Here is a poem by Emily Dickinson which explores even into this world of existentialist action. Written in or about 1861, it reaches across the century to ally itself, not with Heidegger or with Thom Gunn's Heideggerian 'Sad Captains', but with the radical tendencies of some varieties of post-Second World War existentialism:

Unto like Story – Trouble has enticed me –
How Kinsmen fell –
Brothers and Sister – who preferred the Glory –

And their young will
Bent to the Scaffold, or in Dungeons – chanted –
Till God's full time –
When they let go the ignominy – smiling –
And Shame went still –

Unto guessed Crests, my moaning fancy, leads me,
Worn fair
By Heads rejected – in the lower country –
Of honors there –
Such spirit makes her perpetual mention,
That I – grown bold –
Step martial – at my Crucifixion –
As Trumpets – rolled –

Feet, small as mine – have marched in Revolution
Firm to the Drum –
Hands – not so stout – hoisted them – in witness –
When Speech went numb –
Let me not shame their sublime deportments –
Drilled bright –
Beckoning – Etruscan invitation –
Toward Light –

(no. 295)

There is in this poem a deeply moving quality which is very characteristic of some modes of existentialist response – a quality of response to examples of human courage and nobility in action seen against a background of profound ultimate pessimism and emptiness, the emptiness that, expressed at its intensest in Emily Dickinson, is

like Chaos – Stopless – Cool –
Without a Chance, or Spar –
Or even a Report of Land –
To Justify – Despair.

(no. 510)

Against this background what matters most are the 'sublime deportments'; and, by example,

I – grown bold –
Step martial – at my Crucifixion –

Whatever may have been his own personal attitude, Che Guevara, in life and pre-eminently in death, has been seen by many of his admirers as the pattern of the present-day existentialist radical hero, of the 'sublime deportment'. Both the pattern and the response are movingly presented in Emily Dickinson's elegy for the fallen radical heroes. It should be noted, however, that heroic failure, not success, is the source and sustenance of the charisma prized by the existentialist, and can therefore, in some circumstances, be an invitation towards a suicidal foolhardiness in action. A revolutionary movement which succeeded in its aims would be likely soon to lose the revolutionary deportment in the tasks of preserving, consolidating and developing its gains; and this could appear as a betrayal to the existentialist.

Existentialism, as I said, is only one side of Emily Dickinson's many-sidedness, though an important one. I have included this little group of her poems because they seem to me to penetrate remarkably into the essence of an existentialist attitude, and to illuminate vividly some of its obscurer aspects — it is one example of how her poetry can be a guide and lantern to help us understand ourselves more clearly.

If existentialism is an expression of the individual's sense of inner ethical freedom, the ethical awareness and responsibility should be present in all its manifestations. At its best, existentialism is an attempt to liberate and give meaning to the rich inner resources of individual man in a world which denies or obscures real human value. When Iris Murdoch speaks[1] of 'the solitary omnipotent will' at the service of 'the fat relentless ego', of the individual's 'egocentric system of quasi-mechanical energy', she is really speaking of a degraded or fallen existentialism which, from being a liberation of the individual's inner resources of real human value, can become a social force or instrument for the further repression of real human value in the interests of egocentric greed or power; and this too is very characteristic of our age. Iris Murdoch also says[1] 'Kant abolished God and made man God in His stead. We are still living in the age of the Kantian man, or Kantian man—god', or, in another of her phrases, 'the neo-Kantian Lucifer'. It is when existentialism forgets its acute sense of limitation that it lends itself to the emergence of the 'man—god' or 'neo-Kantian Lucifer'; and this apparition also haunts the age, ordinarily in his assumption (which is so often simply taken for granted in our practices) of absolute lordship over nature and nature's creatures to use them as he will. (Human creativity working in and through nature can be a great thing, but only when it is subordinated to a totality which includes but transcends the human; some existentialist philosophy at its deepest recognises something of this.)

I have already tried to indicate, both in the previous chapter and earlier in this, the relation of the real to what presents itself as the real in the consciousness of the age, the consciousness that underlies the existentialist and various other responses. The world as manacle or prison-house of real human value – the world of *Little Dorritt* and *Hard Times* and 'mortal numeral' – imprints itself on this consciousness not just as socio-historic but as an ineluctable natural necessity in which time as a qualitative flowing both in nature and in history is frozen into what Auden in his 'New Year Letter' calls 'The formal logic of the clock', the time of the celestial mechanics to which Emily Dickinson gives such vivid and representative expression; and real value is forced back to its last refuge in the human breast. If I am right in this, it follows that the existentialist response has its *raison d'être* more in historical contingency than in any more ultimate reality of the human situation; and when, in its philosophy, it seeks a more ultimate real, it is a real seen through a veil of contingency.

There is, however, an aspect of existentialism which seems of particular relevance to Emily Dickinson. The French philosopher–critic, Lucien Goldmann, writing of Lukacs and Heidegger,[2] maintains that the true founder of modern existentialism was the young Lukacs in his early book *The Soul and the Forms*, published in 1911. In this presentation, 'authenticity' is achieved and lived in the light of some intense subjective experience and with a consciousness of 'limit' which makes death an ever-present and supreme reality. 'Something lights up, appears like lightning over the banal paths . . .' Lukacs is quoted by Goldmann as saying. 'Death – the limit in itself – constitutes an ever immanent reality. . . . The fact of living this limit constitutes the soul's awakening to consciousness, self-consciousness; it exists because it is limited, and only to the extent in which (and because) it is limited'. In contrast to this, 'Real (inauthentic) life never reaches this limit and only knows death as something terrible, deprived of meaning, which abruptly cuts off its course.' Goldmann himself adds that for Lukacs in 1911 the authentic life 'resides in solitude, in the rejection of all social life with others. It resides in the rejection of history . . . and is opposed to every historical enterprise, whether Shakespeare or Hegel.'

It is almost as if this 1911 Lukacs was writing with Emily Dickinson in mind. For example: 'Death – the limit in itself – constitutes an ever immanent reality.' That death for Emily Dickinson was 'an ever immanent reality' needs no underlining; it is evident throughout her poetry. But now consider this sentence quoted from Lukacs: 'Something lights up, appears like lightning over the banal paths.' In one of her last poems, dating from about the year 1883, Emily Dickinson, looking back from her late period of relatively occasional visitations of major poetic creativity towards her earlier prolific period, describes in similar imagery what seems to be precisely such an experience. Here is the poem:

> The farthest Thunder that I heard
> Was nearer than the Sky
> And rumbles still, though torrid Noons
> Have lain their missiles by –
> The Lightning that preceded it
> Struck no one but myself –
> But I would not exchange the Bolt
> For all the rest of Life –
> Indebtedness to Oxygen
> The Happy may repay,
> But not the obligation
> To Electricity –
> It founds the Homes and decks the Days
> And every clamor bright
> Is but the gleam concomitant
> Of that waylaying Light –
> The Thought is quiet as a Flake –
> A Crash without a Sound,
> How Life's reverberation
> Its Explanation found –
>
> (no. 1581)

A word about the electricity image as she uses it in the poem. For us electricity is the familiar, taken-for-granted electric lighting of ordinary life. But for her, writing when she did, it was primarily the electricity of the lightning flash, and perhaps, in the taming and harnessing of it, something startlingly new and potential in human life; and the need did not arise for her to take special steps, beyond what is provided in the context of the poem as it stands, to guide us away from our present-day stock responses to the term – what to us tends to be a purely technological term could be for her a term of visionary experience. She is contrasting in the poem the 'oxygen' of ordinary everyday life with the 'electricity' of the visionary light.

> It founds the Homes and decks the Days
> And every clamor bright
> Is but the gleam concomitant
> Of that waylaying Light –

'That waylaying Light' — or, as Lukacs put it in the quoted passage, 'Something lights up, appears like lightning over the banal paths.' Everything in vision and creativity that follows is 'but the gleam concomitant' of that experience.

Here, from an earlier period (about 1862), is another poem which perhaps has reference to 'that waylaying Light':

> It struck me — every Day —
> The Lightning was as new
> As if the Cloud that instant slit
> And let the Fire through —
>
> It burned Me — in the Night —
> It Blistered to My Dream —
> It sickened fresh upon my sight —
> With every Morn that came —
>
> I thought that Storm — was brief —
> The Maddest — quickest by —
> But Nature lost the Date of This —
> And left it in the Sky —
>
> (no. 362)

What the experience is that finds expression in the following poem is not stated directly, merely that it is 'as if'; but the imagery of the poem suggests that it could be the 'waylaying Light' itself (the poem is an early one, from about 1858):

> As if I asked a common Alms,
> And in my wondering hand
> A Stranger pressed a Kingdom,
> And I, bewildered, stand —
> As if I asked the Orient
> Had it for me a Morn —
> And it should lift its purple Dikes,
> And shatter me with Dawn!
>
> (no. 323)

I should like to include at this point this attractive little riddle poem, with its culmination in the chiming of the 'Everlasting Clocks' (the 'it's like' of this poem is twin to the 'as if' of the previous one):

It's like the Light –
A fashionless Delight –
It's like the Bee –
A dateless – Melody –

It's like the Woods –
Private – Like the Breeze –
Phraseless – yet it stirs
The proudest Trees –

It's like the Morning –
Best – when it's done –
And the Everlasting Clocks –
Chime – Noon!

(no. 297)

To return to the statement by Goldmann about Lukacs: 'the rejection of all social life with others . . . the rejection of history'. We have already noticed the loss of true history in the chiming of the 'Everlasting Clocks'. Here is a poem of 'the rejection of all social life with others':

The Soul selects her own Society –
Then – shuts the Door –
To her divine Majority –
Present no more –

Unmoved – she notes the Chariots – pausing –
At her low Gate –
Unmoved – an Emperor be kneeling
Upon her Mat –

I've known her – from an ample nation –
Choose One –
Then – close the Valves of her attention –
Like Stone –

(no. 303)

Here is another poem on this theme of solitude, the sort of solitude that is a 'polar privacy':

There is a solitude of space
A solitude of sea

A solitude of death, but these
Society shall be
Compared with that profounder site
That polar privacy
A soul admitted to itself —
Finite infinity.

(no. 1695)

The distinction between authentic and inauthentic living prompts a reflection on our habitual treatment of the lives of some outstanding creative figures. I would substitute here the terms 'ordinary' and 'real' for 'inauthentic' and 'authentic'. The living reality of a true poet, for instance, is surely in his best work as a poet; it is here that he is what he really is, at his real stature, however he may be in his ordinary living. Yet the trend in much present-day biography is to fasten upon the ordinary, the trivia of everyday and the tittle-tattle, and perhaps upon the individual psychological problems of the subject, and to present this, the ordinariness and the psychological twist, as the reality. It is the triumph of the journalistic eye over the philosophic vision, the former driving out the latter like rampant weeds muscling in on the preserves of the precious growths. It is the popular pastime of 'debunking' — some debunking is the casting out of one falseness (hollow outwardness, not inner real) by another falseness; but sometimes it is the destruction of a person's reality by dragging it down into the mess of the ordinary.

If we wish to know and understand the reality of Emily Dickinson, as of all true artists, it is in her best work that we must look, that in which she is striving to realise and express her reality. I conclude this section with this poem of hers:

Of all the Souls that stand create —
I have elected — One —
When Sense from Spirit — files away —
And Subterfuge — is done —
When that which is — and that which was —
Apart — intrinsic — stand —
And this brief Drama in the flesh —
Is shifted — like a Sand —
When Figures show their royal Front —
And Mists — are carved away,
Behold the Atom — I preferred —
To all the lists of Clay!

(no. 664)

NOTES

1. Iris Murdoch, *The Sovereignty of Good* (London: Routledge & Kegan Paul, 1970).
2. Lucien Goldmann, *Lukacs and Heidegger* trans. William Q. Boelhower (London: Routledge & Kegan Paul, 1977).

5

Reality as 'Abyss'

The consciousness which a poet brings to the making of his poetry will normally have two main strands in it. As a member of society he will have a share in the ordinary consciousness of his class or of society as a whole. As a poet, however, he is likely to have a more than ordinary awareness of the inability of the ordinary social consciousness to recognise and articulate its own reality, and of the need to penetrate that reality. I am thinking here, not of an ultimate transcendental reality, though this, whether or not unveiled by his religion, has been a perennial object of the poet's attentions or at least a background presence in his work; but of a more immediate social and human reality – for example, the human reality of any accepted social custom, form or practice which obscures or violates the human; more complexly, all that is expressed and implied in Blake's words, 'blights with plagues the marriage hearse'; more comprehensively, the reality of a money-dominated society uncovered in Shakespeare's *Timon of Athens*. Both the ordinary social or class consciousness and what I might term the reality consciousness have gone to the making of our literature. The proportions have varied, but in all authentic literature the presence of the reality consciousness is crucial. It is because of this presence in it that a work of literature primarily has the possibility of transcending the particular society or class or period from which it sprang, and becoming a permanent living human possession – though, of course, successful realisation by the writer of his theme in art terms is necessary if the possibility is to become actual.

In an age such as ours, with its ever-increasing industrial, economic and technological pressures accompanied by the breakdown of traditional systems of belief, the task of penetrating the veil of contingency which wraps the forms and processes of society, and laying bare something of the structure of the real, confronts the poet with special difficulties beyond those with which his predecessors had to cope; and the task has not been made easier by the kind of consciousness which has typically been brought to it. Inadequate apprehension of the real will not deprive the poet of his insights if he is a true poet, but it will limit or fragment them. Or the reality can insert itself into consciousness as a dimly

66

apprehended unease with ordinary living – this, of course, is something that afflicts many people who are not poets; the poet has the advantage of being able to articulate and elaborate his unease, and perhaps raise it to a nightmarish intensity.

Auden, in his 'New Year Letter', speaks of

> the abyss
> That always lies just underneath
> Our jolly picnic on the heath
> Of the agreeable, where we bask,
> Agreed on what we will not ask,
> Bland, sunny and adjusted by
> The light of the accepted lie.

In 'New Year Letter' Auden tried to explore the immediate reality of the abyss and reveal it as it is, shorn of its qualities of abyss and menace. (The further 'no-man-fathomed' depths beyond the immediate reality are another story.)

A systematic and coherent exploration, such as Auden's, of the immediate underlying reality is unusual in our poetry. For the most part, including in its Romantic expressions (for example, in early Wordsworth and Coleridge, and in Shelley and Keats), our literature since the decisive seventeenth-century changes has been a literature of the liberal consciousness – and of the disillusions of that consciousness – the consciousness which at its best has been the enlightenment, the humanism and idealism of society, and defender and asserter of its proclaimed values, while yet retaining in its idealistic versions the general characteristics and assumptions of the ordinary social consciousness. This means that, whereas an earlier consciousness might have been able to measure its society in terms of an awareness based outside the society, in a moral or spiritual order set above the temporal order, a typical liberal consciousness could only assess its society in terms of an idealistic or more sensitively human version of itself – it could, for example, arraign society for imperfectly embodying in its actual forms and practices its own proclaimed values, or (and here the literature of the liberal consciousness achieved its richest and deepest, though still insecurely based, insights) for neglecting or violating or excluding the real human content of its values; but, of its very nature, it could not grasp and articulate its reality in its totality. Yet the tensions between the liberal vision and the social actuality provided, within the limitation, very considerable scope for the literature of the period – for example, in its

Wordsworthian, its Shelleyan and its critical–realist modes.

Beyond these normal tensions, asserting itself typically as crisis – an insertion of the seemingly inexplicable and irrational into the rational but contingent order and its consciousness – was a further and growing dimension in the pressures of underlying reality. It is no accident that the Modernist movement should have emerged towards the end of the nineteenth century among those most sensitively attuned to these seismic pressures. Through the many and varied manifestations and fashions of Modernism, it is possible to see the Modernist movement, in its initial impulses, its primary *raison d'être*, as an expression of the liberal consciousness in crisis. Reality felt as crisis or 'abyss', as a spectral irrationality haunting the rational and intelligible; reality disguised in consciousness as a crisis of traditional art forms and ways of thinking, feeling and observing.

I have described Emily Dickinson as centrally representative of the consciousness of the age. An exploration such as Auden's in 'New Year Letter', with its central awareness of qualitative historic pressures on a man-made order subject to laws of history but understanding itself under terms analogous to laws of nature, was outside her field of vision; but she was no stranger to the further depths of the abyss beyond the immediate reality. The mind 'tilling its abyss' is a phrase she uses in one of her poems. But whereas Auden places the abyss under the 'picnic on the heath', suggesting social insecurity, Emily Dickinson finds it in the individual human consciousness and in nature – in the human soul with its 'Cellars', its 'Caverns' and 'Corridors' and 'Subterranean Freight'; and in the 'unknown modes of being' of a nature that, like the human mind, cannot be confined within the stereotypes and over-simplifications of our ordinary consciousness.

'What Terror would enthrall the Street' she says in one poem

> Could Countenance disclose
> The Subterranean Freight
> The Cellars of the Soul –
> (no. 1225)

In another poem she speaks of

> The Horror not to be surveyed –
> But skirted in the Dark –
> With Consciousness suspended –
> And Being under Lock –

I fear me this — is Loneliness —
The Maker of the soul
Its Caverns and its Corridors
Illuminate — or seal —

(no. 777)

Here now is a poem of the skirting of the abyss with 'Being under Lock':

There is a pain — so utter —
It swallows substance up —
Then covers the Abyss with Trance —
So Memory can step
Around — across — upon it —
As one within a Swoon —
Goes safely — where an open eye —
Would Drop Him — Bone by Bone.

(no. 599)

Perhaps Emily Dickinson felt that she was trying to solder the abyss with air, when she wrote the following, very perspicacious, little poem:

To fill a Gap
Insert the Thing that caused it —
Block it up
With Other — and 'twill yawn the more —
You cannot solder an Abyss
With Air.

(no. 546)

The message of this little poem is surely deep and clear, and is especially apt for an age such as ours in coping adequately with the pressures of underlying reality on the age.

Consider now this poem of the 'Pit':

A Pit — but Heaven over it —
And Heaven beside, and Heaven abroad,
And yet a Pit —
With Heaven over it.

To stir would be to slip —
To look would be to drop —

To dream — to sap the Prop
That holds my chances up.
Ah! Pit! With Heaven over it!

The depth is all my thought —
I dare not ask my feet —
'Twould start us where we sit
So straight you'd scarce suspect
It was a Pit — with fathoms under it —
Its Circuit just the same.
Seed — summer — tomb —
Whose Doom to whom?

(no. 1712)

This, surely, is a fascinating little poem. Human life — or, rather,
consciousness, the poet's consciousness — seems to dwell in it between
two dimensions of felt reality — 'Heaven' and the 'Pit'. But towards the
end of the poem a third dimension seems to be emerging — an implicit
recognition of nature, with its stabilities and cyclical recurrences, as man's
ground of being and ultimate security amidst life's insecurities and the
thrusts of consciousness into dimensions above and below. 'Seed —
summer — tomb' — birth — maturity — death — and yet, under the stabilities,
the felt reality of the 'Pit', the realm of 'unknown modes of being',
remaining unexorcised. At least, I think these are implications of the
poem, with its rather cryptic concluding lines.

In the following poem the abyss or pit under the surface life resolves
into a well:

What mystery pervades a well!
That water lives so far —
A neighbor from another world
Residing in a jar

Whose limit none have ever seen,
But just his lid of glass —
Like looking every time you please
In an abyss's face!

The grass does not appear afraid,
I often wonder he
Can stand so close and look so bold
At what is awe to me.

Related somehow they may be,
The sedge stands next the sea –
Where he is floorless
And does no timidity betray

But nature is a stranger yet;
The ones that cite her most
Have never passed her haunted house,
Nor simplified her ghost.

To pity those that know her not
Is helped by the regret
That those who know her, know her less
The nearer her they get.

(no. 1400)

The well with only its surface water, its 'lid of glass', visible to ordinary observation, 'whose limit none have ever seen', is an image of nature; only by implication in the poem is it also an image of the human mind. Both the poet and the grass at the well's edge look into the hidden depths of their being, but the grass feels neither fear nor the poet's awe – fear and awe are the privilege of consciousness. But in this poem fear of the unknown depths is mastered; the awe remains, but with it a lucid understanding and imaginative realisation. The poet might easily have applied the well image solely or primarily to the human mind with its depths below the threshold of ordinary consciousness – it would have been appropriate, and an obvious temptation. That she located the unknown depths outside the mind, in objective nature, shows a profounder insight – a recognition of nature as man's ground of being and maker and well-head of the mind's own depths and inner riches. This, I think, is the reality of the abyss which the poem conveys; though the ultimate question remains, the 'Riddle' through which, 'at the last, Sagacity must go' (no. 501).

The picture of the grass and the poet at the well's edge, the grass unafraid, the poet with her burden of consciousness, expresses a recovered unity with nature at a high level of human awareness and understanding, the poet fulfilling her role as nature's consciousness and tongue. Nevertheless, the discontinuities as well as the continuities between the natural order and the human order remain. The mind that knows, being separate, necessarily falsifies nature in the process of knowing her; and 'nature is a stranger yet'.

those who know her, know her less
The nearer her they get.

Here is another of her poems — a poem of human discontinuity in the midst of nature:

It makes no difference abroad —
The Seasons — fit — the same —
The Mornings blossom into Noons —
And split their Pods of Flame —

Wild flowers — kindle in the Woods —
The Brooks slam — all the Day —
No Black bird bates his Banjo —
For passing Calvary —

Auto da Fe — and Judgment —
Are nothing to the Bee —
His separation from His Rose —
To Him — sums Misery —

(no. 620)

Compare the above poem with this stanza from another of her poems:

The Sun, as common, went abroad,
The flowers, accustomed, blew,
As if no soul the solstice passed
That maketh all things new —

(no. 322)

We have here the human counterpart of nature's well. In any adequate recapture of unity between the natural and the human orders, both dimensions must be dynamically present, as, supremely, in Shakespeare, in the poetry that soars far beyond the limitations of the characters and plots. Emily Dickinson is pre-eminently a poet of the human dimension, of man's adventure in his apartness from nature and specifically of his modern situation in the Western order; yet recognising in nature, in her deepest insights into nature, his necessary ground of being.

Here to end this chapter, is another of her poems:

On this long storm the Rainbow rose —
On this late Morn — the Sun

The clouds – like listless Elephants –
Horizons – straggled down –

The Birds rose smiling, in their nests –
The gales – indeed – were done –
Alas, how heedless were the eyes –
On whom the summer shone!

The quiet nonchalance of death –
No Daybreak – can bestir –
The slow – Archangel's syllables
Must awaken her!

                       (no. 194)

6

'Not Joy, But a Decree'

Our journey had advanced –
Our feet were almost come
To that odd Fork in Being's Road –
Eternity – by Term –

Our pace took sudden awe –
Our feet – reluctant – led –
Before – were Cities – but Between –
The Forest of the Dead –

Retreat – was out of Hope –
Behind – a Sealed Route –
Eternity's White Flag – Before –
And God – at every Gate –

(no. 615)

This poem of Emily Dickinson's falls within the great tradition. Its God is the God of 'Eternity', and 'Eternity' is the goal of 'Being's' pilgrimage through time. Her God of the new scientific and social order, however, is 'God of Width'; 'His Scene, Infinity'; His 'Continent', 'All Latitudes'. These phrases are taken from three of her poems, written at different times. In another poem she speaks of

the Stupendous Vision
Of His diameters.

(no. 802)

His time is the clock-time whose ultimate in death is mere cessation or the passage from 'mortal numeral' to unresolved particle in infinite space. When time is spatialised in the clock-face and the celestial mechanics, and reduced to endless repetitiveness, it resolves itself into infinity, infinite space; not into its transcendence in eternity – infinity is a quantitative concept, eternity a qualitative one.

The relation of the human not only to society, but to the universe as unveiled by modern science, and to its God, was a central preoccupation of Emily Dickinson's poetry, and a source of some of her finest poems. We have seen in earlier sections something of this preoccupation and of its ramifications. In this section I want to look a little further at her confrontations with and responses to this implacable necessity as it presented itself to her and to the consciousness of the age. The central problem was the breakdown of the traditional spiritual order, and the loss of the sanctions, values and relationships that depended on this order. 'The abdication of Belief', Emily Dickinson said, 'makes the behavior small'. The present is perhaps even more the time of the small behaviour than when she wrote. For her, as for many others in her day, the abdication of belief was a searing crisis of the human spirit. Philip Larkin, I suppose, is our chief modern poet of the small behaviour (I do not mean by this that he is a small poet). Emily Dickinson is pre-eminently the poet of the traumatic experience, of the direct confrontations and responses.

Beyond all the particular beliefs, religious forms, dogmas, philosophies and superstitions in which it has received more or less imperfect expression, men have held that transcending the world of nature, but underlying and informing it, there is an ultimate reality which is also present in ourselves and is our ground of being. This, or some version of it, is the vision of reality and of the real human situation which has been a sustaining force through the ages and gives to human life its sense of meaning and value amidst the actualities of ordinary life. Here is a poem by Emily Dickinson which expresses this sense of the relationship of the human to its own reality, to its ground of being, and what it means, and what its loss would mean:

Empty my Heart, of Thee —
Its single Artery —
Begin, and leave Thee out —
Simply Extinction's Date —

Much Billow hath the Sea —
One Baltic — They —
Subtract Thyself, in play,
And not enough of me
Is left — to put away —
'Myself' meant Thee —

Erase the Root — not Tree —
Thee — then — no me —

> The Heavens stripped –
> Eternity's vast pocket, picked –
> (no. 587)

The severing of the artery, of the root, the subtraction of the wave's Baltic – these are the operations that the age performed upon the consciousness. Here is a poem of response to the surgery, to the 'stripped Heavens' – it seems to me a great one:

> Superfluous were the Sun
> When Excellence be dead
> He were superfluous every Day
> For every Day be said
>
> That syllable whose Faith
> Just saves it from Despair
> And whose 'I'll meet You' hesitates
> If Love inquire 'Where'?
>
> Upon His dateless Fame
> Our Periods may lie
> As Stars that drop anonymous
> From an abundant sky.
> (no. 999)

Faith hesitates and is lost when pressed for a convincing answer. We have seen in an earlier section how time as a qualitative flowing is annulled in the consciousness in the spatialised time of the celestial mechanics. In its cosmic dimension time thus conceived is timeless (the sun's 'dateless Fame') – in other words, it also annuls itself as time. But in its human dimension its aspect as time is inexorable – man's subordination to clock and calendar is absolute. At first in the poem the emergent 'Despair' is immersed in the deeper grammatical layers of the language. Emily Dickinson uses these deeper layers for an introspective exploring mode of expression, the poet talking to herself, developing what is germinal and as yet undetermined in her consciousness into the spoken word which then breaks through to the clear light of the indicative as a musical theme might change from a minor to a major key. Sometimes she reverses the process, drawing back from the indicative to introspective exploring in the deeper layers.

The cutting of the root or artery reduces individual man to 'mortal numeral', to mere instrumentality; or, where consciousness is intense, to an atom of acute self-awareness confronting an alien universe.

> To my quick ear the Leaves – conferred –
> The Bushes – they were Bells –
> I could not find a Privacy
> From Nature's sentinels –
>
> In Cave if I presumed to hide
> The Walls – begun to tell –
> Creation seemed a mighty Crack –
> To make me visible –
>
> (no. 891)

Here now is a poem of the solitary soul adrift in a universe where it can find no ground of being, not even a toehold for human value – 'mortal numeral' is still an isolated numeral, 'A Speck upon a Ball':

> I saw no Way – The Heavens were stitched –
> I felt the Columns close –
> The Earth reversed her Hemispheres –
> I touched the Universe –
>
> And back it slid – and I alone –
> A Speck upon a Ball –
> Went out upon Circumference –
> Beyond the Dip of Bell –
>
> (no. 378)

Here is another poem:

> Departed – to the Judgment –
> A Mighty Afternoon –
> Great Clouds – like Ushers – leaning –
> Creation – looking on –
>
> The Flesh – Surrendered – Cancelled –
> The Bodiless – begun –
> Two Worlds – like Audiences – disperse –
> And leave the Soul – alone –
>
> (no. 524)

'Those dying then', Emily Dickinson says elsewhere,

> Knew where they went —
> They went to God's Right Hand —
> (no. 1551)

But now, when the summons is to the cold, impersonal, though perhaps just, Newtonian heavens? Here, in this poem, is one answer; as, in the previous, is another.

The new concepts of order, in the heavens as on earth, do not necessarily abolish God from the consciousness, but they do make Him unfit for human companionship and comfort in the traditional ways. In Emily Dickinson's words, He is now 'Not Joy, but a Decree'. Here is the poem from which these words are taken:

> Expanse cannot be lost —
> Not Joy, but a Decree
> Is Deity —
> His Scene, Infinity —
> Whose rumor's Gate was shut so tight
> Before my Beam was sown,
> Not even a Prognostic's push
> Could make a Dent thereon —
>
> The World that thou hast opened
> Shuts for thee,
> But not alone,
> We all have followed thee —
> Escape more slowly
> To thy Tracts of Sheen
> The Tent is listening,
> But the Troops are gone!
> (no. 1584)

It is the shutting down of the traditional order in the new emergent consciousness of our age. The 'Tent' of the traditional order is still there, but emptied of its content. The crucial changes that made the 'Deity', insofar as it spared Him at all, impersonal and remote, and shut His 'rumor's Gate', took place, of course, well before her day ('Before my Beam was sown'); but it was only in her day, and in the decades immediately after, that the realisation reached crisis point in the consciousness. But this poem is not an uncontrolled expression of or reaction to a sense of crisis, but a controlled assessment and presentation of the situation – as a good poem, even of what is felt as acute crisis, should be.

It is interesting to speculate why what was implicit in the Copernican –Newtonian system from the outset only reached crisis point towards the end of the nineteenth century. The answer, I think, is to be found not primarily in the Newtonian system itself, but in the socio-economic order that at birth twinned with the Newtonian system and grew up with it; it was here that, since the beginnings of the Industrial Revolution, the latent pressures in the new order were growing rapidly until they began to assert themselves critically – the accompanying sense of cosmic alienation in its intensified form was more a consequence than the prime cause of the very real experience of social alienation. Since Emily Dickinson's day, of course, the Newtonian system, which had seemed so unassailable, has been profoundly modified by new developments in physical science, inserting into the mechanics of the system, amongst other changes, new concepts of process and of laws governing process; but the central unresolved problem remains – the place of human value in the cosmic process as, primarily, in a social order which is also under pressure from the invasive realities of process (historical process, in this instance) but which is so far resisting the changes these pressures would involve.

A further note on the God who is now 'Not Joy, but a Decree'. That He is a God of 'Decree' is not, of course, anything new. He has always been that in the traditional Christian order, but with this vital difference, that 'Joy' and 'Decree' were not antithetical but complementary – 'Joy' lay in submission to divine 'Decree' ('His will is our peace'). There was also 'Joy' in the possibility or hope of a personal relationship with this God, whether directly or mediated through the Son. Though of course the 'Joy' in the relationship was not simple and unalloyed – the God of 'Joy', of love, was also the God of earthquake and tempest, the God of Gerard Manley Hopkins' 'The Wreck of the Deutschland':

> Thou art lightning and love, I found it, a winter and warm;
> Father and fondler of heart thou hast wrung:
> Hast thy dark descending and most art merciful then.

A crucial event in changing all this was the Copernican revolution, which displaced earth and man from the centre of the universe, and therefore from being self-evidently the centre of God's concern. Here again,

however, the primary and decisive factor in changing men's consciousness was not the cosmic picture in itself, but the social experience – the
ever-intensifying pressures of a social, economic and technological order
which paradoxically both set free the individual from old constraints and
at the same time subordinated him to the overall necessities of the system,
reducing real human value to instrumentality and 'thingness'. At the
dawn of the nineteenth century it was the element of freedom in the new
order that was fervently proclaimed, though with warning signals from
the more far-sighted (Wordsworth's 'shades of the prison-house');
towards the end of the century it was the humanly reductive element that
was pressing most critically on the consciousness. We have already seen
in Emily Dickinson's poetry examples of her acute awareness and
understanding of this element in our modern situation – the reduction of
man to 'mortal numeral', 'Limit – how deep a bleeding', the paradox of
'Manacle' and 'Freedom':

> God of the Manacle
> As of the Free.
> (no. 728)

What the Copernican picture did was to add a cosmic dimension, and an
apparent sanction, to the very real social experience, converting the
experience from a historical phenomenon into what seemed a natural
necessity to the consciousness. A divine plan which apparently so
transcended earth's and man's demoted status in the universe might not
after all be a source of joy and comfort to man in his necessary submission
to the plan. Emily Dickinson questions the God of this order thus in one of
her poems:

> Hast thou Delight or Fear
> Or Longing – and is that for us
> Or values more severe?
> (no. 1689)

Here is another poem, in which she explores something of what might
be involved in these 'values more severe':

> It's easy to invent a Life –
> God does it – every Day –
> Creation – but the Gambol
> Of His Authority –

> It's easy to efface it –
> The thrifty Deity
> Could scarce afford Eternity
> To Spontaneity –
>
> The Perished Patterns murmur –
> But His Perturbless Plan
> Proceed – inserting Here – a Sun –
> There – leaving out a Man –
> > (no. 724)

'The Perished Patterns', or, to quote these other lines of hers on the human ephemera of the universe,

> Stars that drop anonymous
> From an abundant sky.
> > (no. 999)

There is little left of the traditional Christian God in the God of this poem. But there is something in Him that is slightly reminiscent of Gloucester's gods in *King Lear*:

> As flies to wanton boys, are we to the gods;
> They kill us for their sport.

But whereas Gloucester's gods are unpredictable and brutally sporty despots, pre-Christian feudal or pre-feudal, Emily Dickinson's poem imposes on the transcendental a very different social pattern – rational, mathematical–mechanistic, technical, using people as means not ends, governed by strict economic law –

> The thrifty Deity
> Could scarce afford Eternity
> To Spontaneity –

and yet – and this is a crucial point – with its underlying creative source and pressures unable to be contained within the prevailing rationality:

> Creation – but the Gambol
> Of His Authority –

I called this a crucial point – for it is here that the all-encompassing prevailing type of rationality partly breaks down under the pressures of creative spontaneity; an insertion of creative process into a system whose mathematical–rational pattern resists process; a 'Gambol' in an otherwise 'Perturbless Plan', for the spontaneous unchecked and wasteful outpouring of life is hardly, on the face of it, an example of good rational planning. An analogy in the socio-economic twin sphere would be the pressures of underlying historical process on the system, with a possibility of creative newness breaking through the resistances, but leading primarily to crisis, a seeming irrationality infecting the ordered rationality of the system.

Here is another vision of the king of the great spaces:

> All Circumstances are the Frame
> In which His Face is set –
> All Latitudes exist for His
> Sufficient Continent –
>
> The Light His Action, and the Dark
> The Leisure of His Will –
> In Him Existence serve or set
> A Force illegible
>
> > (no. 820)

He is also king of the workaday world of 'Circumstance', of 'Existence' serving and setting illegibly like the anonymous falling stars.

Consider now this poem of God's procedures and men's – it is, surely, a notable example of insight and understanding at a philosophical level, of thinking fused into poetry:

> 'Tis One by One – the Father counts –
> And then a Tract between
> Set Cypherless – to teach the Eye
> The Value of its Ten –
>
> Until the peevish Student
> Acquire the Quick of Skill –
> Then Numerals are dowered back –
> Adorning all the Rule –
>
> 'Tis mostly Slate and Pencil –
> And Darkness on the School

Distracts the Children's fingers —
Still the Eternal Rule

Regards least Cypherer alike
With Leader of the Bank —
And every separate Urchin's Sum —
Is fashioned for his hand —

(no. 545)

Although God uses the methods of the prevailing socio-economic order —
of the counting, statistical Benthamite society — He nevertheless leaves
some open spaces, cypherless tracts amidst the counting, the 'Gambol' in
the mathematics, for the imagination to enter. The 'peevish Student', the
'Children', the 'Cypherer' and the 'Urchin', who systematically close these
open spaces, are of course the established intellectual elite of the age,
who, usurping the authority of God the 'Leader of the Band' and making
the human mind the lawgiver to nature, have ordered the how of things as
we know them into a system 'fashioned for his hand' (fashioned for the
prevailing human order), and presented this as the reality.

In this next poem the Newtonian heavens begin to shine transcendentally, 'As an Astral Hall':

Lightly stepped a yellow star
To its lofty place —
Loosed the Moon her silver hat
From her lustral Face —

All of Evening softly lit
As an Astral Hall —
Father, I observed to Heaven,
You are punctual.

(no. 1672)

I have included this little poem as a prelude to the following:

Trusty as the stars
Who quit their shining working
Prompt as when I lit them
In Genesis' new house,
Durable as dawn
Whose antiquated blossom

> Makes a world's suspense
> Perish and rejoice.
>
> (no. 1369)

The stress here is all on the reassurance that flows from the reliability and precision of the celestial order — the trust, the durability, and the punctuality that guarantees the trust. Beauty and rejoicing also flow from the primary mechanics of the system — the 'God of Decree' is again also the 'God of Joy'; not only the God of quantity, of latitudes and diameters, but the God of quality, of quality breaking through from quantity; and, in and through nature with its stabilities and cyclical recurrences, our ground of being and ultimate security amidst life's insecurities and deprivations. The paradisal state of the little stone

> Fulfilling absolute Decree
> In casual simplicity
>
> (no. 1510)

is recovered in this poem, though the poet has journeyed through the regions we have seen in this and in other sections.

This is another of Emily Dickinson's later poems, another of her late returns in short poems to what I earlier called the paradisal substratum of human experience, with its experienced reality of the accosting power, the 'Garment of Surprise'. 'By his intrusion, God is known', she says in another poem. It was the only adequate answer she could give to the questionings raised in other of her poems; perhaps, when philosophy has done its best to negotiate the 'Riddle' through which 'Sagacity must go', the only persuasive answer possible in an age when 'rumor's Gate' (revelation) is shut tight — the experience at least is real, the primal and perennially recoverable real of man's place in the universe, whether or not we find in its accosting power and 'Garment of Surprise' the breathing presence of the God who is both 'Joy' and 'Decree'.

7

The Realism of the 'Solid Town'

By way of transition from what has gone before to the theme of this chapter, I should like to begin with this poem of Emily Dickinson's:

> I started Early – Took My Dog –
> And visited the Sea –
> The Mermaids in the Basement
> Came out to look at me –
>
> And Frigates – in the Upper Floor
> Extended Hempen Hands –
> Presuming Me to be a Mouse –
> Aground – upon the Sands –
>
> But no Man moved Me – till the Tide
> Went past my simple Shoe –
> And past my Apron – and my Belt
> And past my Bodice – too –
>
> And made as He would eat me up –
> As wholly as a Dew
> Upon a Dandelion's Sleeve –
> And then – I started – too –
>
> And He – He followed – close behind –
> I felt His Silver Heel
> Upon my Ankle – Then my Shoes
> Would overflow with Pearl –
>
> Until We met the Solid Town –
> No One He seemed to know –
> And bowing – with a Mighty look –
> At me – The Sea withdrew –

(no. 520)

James Reeves, in his introduction to his selection of Emily Dickinson's poetry, says of this 'extraordinary and tantalizing poem' (as he describes it): 'It is evident that here the sea represents some overwhelming force, of great destructive power. . . . What begins in a playful vein concludes as a pursuit to the death. It is only when she reaches the solid familiarity of home, the reassurance of the town she knows so well, that the pursuit ends.' I am not sure about the appropriateness of the term 'playful' as applied to the beginning of the poem. The lightness of the opening (light rather than playful) is an integral and calculated part of the serious purpose of the whole, and introduces several essential properties of the poem. Perhaps we can interpret the 'Mermaids in the Basement' as the deluding phantoms or sirens of the deep, luring to destruction; and the 'Frigates in the Upper Floor' as the great masters, a Dante, a Shakespeare, who have plumbed and mastered the depths of human experience and can safely ride the deep, extending 'Hempen Hands' to the small isolated figure caught up in the destructive elements. Even the dog, which enters the poem only to disappear from it immediately, has its significance – the significance is perhaps in the disappearance itself, the breakdown, when the situation begins to get serious, of the substitute companionship ('no Man moved Me') demanded of the dog in the absence of the real human companionships and support that the town might provide.

'The solid familiarity of home, the reassurance of the town she knows so well' – yes, but of course the poet's real relationships with the 'Solid Town' were more complex than that; it is not a mere homesick child who is heading for the town after receiving a bad fright which any sympathetic adult can help to dispel, though the poem does seem to be cast in that familiar mould. The 'Dog', the 'Mermaids', the 'Frigates', the 'Mouse', the 'Apron', 'Belt' and 'Bodice', the 'Silver Heel', the 'Shoes' overflowing with 'Pearl', the bad fright and the race for home – all these seem to form a familiar age-old pattern, though given a new content and depth of meaning. If the relics of childhood are still present though transcended in the poem, that only adds to the poem's profound insight, expressing an abiding reality of the human consciousness.

My purpose in this section is to look at Emily Dickinson's poetry of the 'Solid Town', her work as a realist poet of the human social order. This poem of the retreat to the 'Solid Town' only takes us to the threshold of this. Before crossing that threshold, I want to look a little further at the picture presented in the poem, of the poet alone with her dog outside the town's limits, pursued by the rising tide of consciousness or (to change the metaphor to that of another of her poems) by 'That awful stranger Consciousness', the presence whom she is trying to exorcise or master through the return to the town.

> I do not know the man so bold
> He dare in lonely Place
> That awful stranger Consciousness
> Deliberately face —
>
> (no. 1323)

a 'stranger' because, as she says elsewhere:

> A doubt if it be Us
> Assists the staggering Mind
> In an extremer Anguish
> Until it footing find.
>
> An Unreality is lent,
> A merciful Mirage
> That makes the living possible
> While it suspends the lives.
>
> (no. 859)

The theme of the exorcising or mastering of consciousness is taken up again in another poem:

> Me from Myself — to banish —
> Had I Art —
> Impregnable my Fortress
> Unto All Heart —
>
> But since Myself — assault Me —
> How have I peace
> Except by subjugating
> Consciousness?
>
> And since We're mutual Monarch
> How this be
> Except by Abdication —
> Me — of Me?
>
> (no. 642)

If the flight to the 'Solid Town', the 'Abdication — Me — of Me', was a retreat, it was a retreat to the real from an excess of subjective response to the real or to what presented itself to the consciousness as such; not a flight from reality, but an illuminating by reality of the 'Caverns' and 'Corridors' opened up in the following poem (it is the loneliness that is stressed here — we have already seen it in the situation, the poet alone with her dog and the 'awful stranger'):

> The Loneliness One dare not sound —
> And would as soon surmise
> As in its Grave go plumbing
> To ascertain the size —
>
> The Loneliness whose worst alarm
> Is lest itself should see —
> And perish from before itself
> For just a scrutiny —
>
> The Horror not to be surveyed —
> But skirted in the Dark —
> With Consciousness suspended —
> And Being under Lock —
>
> I fear me this — is Loneliness —
> The Maker of the soul
> Its Caverns and its Corridors
> Illuminate — or seal —
>
> (no. 777)

To return to the quotation from Theodore Roszak in my Introduction, this is a poetry of 'the abyss' (the 'awful stranger' poem contains the phrase, the mind 'tilling its abyss'), a poetry that has 'with Conrad's Mr Kurtz, looked into the heart of darkness and seen "horror"'; yet only a staging-post in her explorations of the real.

Just as she turned to nature for meaning, value and reassurance in this predicament, so she turned for these to the human social order; and the task was as complex in the latter sphere as in the former, and more intractable. For while the sense of cosmic meaninglessness and abandonment might be overcome in the end, in ways we have seen, the realities of social alienation remain realities — though, being historical realities, they are not of the order of natural necessity, but subject to the laws of history.

A realist poetry of human society invites comparison with the realist novel. Emily Dickinson has her own verse comment on this:

'Tis Fiction's – to dilute to Plausibility
Our Novel – When 'tis small enough
To Credit – 'Tisn't true!

(no. 669)

In making this comment she was, of course, measuring the traditional
novel as she knew it against her own experience and practice as a poet –
the poet who had explored the depths and ranges of experience that lie
beyond the limits of the 'Solid Town' against the novel that normally kept
within those limits. Before proceeding, I want to look a little further at the
relation of poetry to the novel – in particular, to the nineteenth-century
realist novel at its best.

It has been contended that the true heirs of the great poets of the past
are not the poets but the great novelists – notably perhaps, in our
language, Dickens, George Eliot, James, Conrad, D.H. Lawrence. If this is
so, or appears to be, it should be interesting to try to discover why.
There are two typical limitations in modern poetry (apart from the
normal limitations of a decadent end to a great era and the early problems
of innovation) that perhaps lie behind this judgment. One is the
increasing restriction, under pressure from the novel and prose drama, of
the realm of poetry to the short lyric. The other is the fragmentation of
insight in poetry. Now fragmentation of insight is not a necessary
concomitant of lyric shortness (neither George Herbert nor Hopkins, for
example, are poets of fragmented insight). In general, it can be said that
where an underlying coherence of world-view or vision (or at least, as we
have seen in the case of Emily Dickinson, the attempt to achieve such a
coherence in the difficult modern conditions) is lacking, the poet's insights
will necessarily be fragmented; and, further, that fragmentation of insight
is the crucial factor that makes for limitation in the scope of poetry. If,
then, there is truth in the view that the novelists, not the poets, are the
true heirs of the poets of the past, it is, I think, not primarily because of the
increasing restriction of poetry to the short lyric as such, but because of
the fragmentation of insight in so much of the poetry. It is the poet's
whole work – or, rather, his totality of vision or awareness as explored
and presented in his work – that must be matched against the
achievement of the novelist; and such a poetry, so regarded, will not fail
to reassert the traditional primacy of poetry. But in a poetry of
fragmented insights, the sum total of the work can never add up to a true
totality. The situation is enshrined in the cult of the anthology piece – the
apotheosis of the short poem as an isolated event. It is from apparent
participation in this situation that I have been trying to rescue Emily
Dickinson in this study.

The limitations of a fragmented insight into underlying reality are less obviously restrictive on the novelist because he is able to integrate these insights into a coherent presentation of the visible social scene, with all its teeming life and interrelatedness, which of course is not possible for a poetry of lyric shortness. Yet it is no accident that, to elicit and explore the 'Central Mood'of the age, it has been necessary to go, not to the great novelists of the age, but to a poet. This, I think, is the inner meaning of Emily Dickinson's little verse comment.

In Chapter 5 of this study it was suggested that, whereas an earlier consciousness might have been able to measure its society in terms of an awareness based outside the society, in a moral or spiritual order set above the temporal order, a typical modern consciousness (liberal humanist in its prevailing modes) could only assess its society in terms of an idealistic or more sensitively human version of itself — it could, for example, arraign society for imperfectly embodying in its actual forms and practices its own proclaimed values, or for neglecting or violating or excluding the real human content of its values; but, of its very nature, it could not grasp and articulate its reality in totality. If this analysis is valid, it should help to explain both the strengths and the limitations of the great realist novel of the nineteenth century. The glory of this novel was in its penetration into real moral and human values in terms of which it weighed the actualities of the social life it portrayed on its large canvas. Its limitation was in its inability to recognise adequately the presence and real nature of the deeper underlying pressures of reality which towards the end of the century were to produce a crisis of response in literature and the arts. Emily Dickinson's verse comment correctly pinpoints the limitations of the novel of her day in contrast to her own work as a poet; but as for its strengths — she herself in some of her work displayed these qualities in a form of realism which, though familiar in the novel, was new in the poetry of the age (except, a little later, in Hardy — though what in Emily Dickinson, underlying the purely social situation, was 'Manacle', cosmic and social, in Hardy was usually expressed as irony, also cosmic as well as social). In these modes, she was the poet of the insights of the realist novel; but, lacking the novel's larger canvas, of these insights reduced to their essence and transmuted into lyric.

Here, for example, are two realist poems on the theme of marriage. First, this:

> She rose to His Requirement — dropt
> The Playthings of Her Life
> To take the honorable Work
> Of Woman, and of Wife —

If ought She missed in Her new Day
Of Amplitude, or Awe —
Or first Prospective — Or the Gold
In using, wear away,

It lay unmentioned — as the Sea
Develop Pearl, and Weed,
But only to Himself — be known
The Fathoms they abide —
                              (no. 732)

As the poet—explorer of the hidden depths of the consciousness, the poet knew, better perhaps than the novelist, how many fathoms deep; and knew, too, how much of what developed from this situation of the human was 'Weed' not 'Pearl' or 'Pearl' become 'Weed'.

I gave myself to Him —
And took Himself, for Pay,
The solemn contract of a Life
Was ratified, this way —

The Wealth might disappoint —
Myself a poorer prove
Than this great Purchaser suspect
The Daily Own — of Love

Depreciate the Vision —
But till the Merchant buy —
Still Fable — in the Isles of Spice —
The subtle Cargoes — lie —

At least — 'tis Mutual — Risk —
Some — found it — Mutual Gain —
Sweet Debt of Life — Each Night to owe —
Insolvent — every Noon —
                              (no. 580)

The economic, property, basis of the marriage institution, and the egotistical possessiveness that can be the reality of a seeming selflessness, are hinted at in the language of the poem, though not explicitly developed in its substance. What is involved in the realistic scrutiny of the poem is the fate of the real value relationship, the 'bright incipience' expressed in the beautiful lyricism of

> But till the Merchant buy –
> Still Fable – in the Isles of Spice –
> The subtle Cargoes – lie –

(I have borrowed the phrase 'bright incipience' from Philip Larkin's poem, 'Love Songs in Age'). I said 'the real value relationship', for what is expressed in these lines is not illusion in opposition to reality but something that belongs to the real of the human essence, of a different order from the social realities to which it is subjected when the 'merchant' purchases the intrinsic value and reduces it to a possession made contractually binding under the prevailing laws and institutions of society.

This type of social realist poetry has remained exceptional in our modern poetry until after the Second World War, since when it has had some stirrings. Whether or not Larkin would have acknowledged the ancestry, I think Emily Dickinson can be clearly seen, not just as a predecessor, but as model in this field – it is yet another respect in which she is a representative poet of the age. This post-Second World War phenomenon is worth looking at for a moment. In what follows in the next paragraph, I am thinking primarily of the English scene – it will, I think, help to explain what a number of critics have felt as a serious limitation in much English poetry of the period, contrasting unfavourably with, for example, American poetry of the same period.[1]

I said earlier that most of our literature since the decisive seventeenth-century changes has been a literature of the liberal consciousness, not only of its optimism, but of its disillusions and despairs and, towards the end of the nineteeenth century, of its crisis. After the partial interregnum of the 1930s, most, and the most characteristic, of our poetry since the end of the Second World War has again been a poetry of the liberal consciousness. But in some ways it has been a revivified, almost a renascent, liberalism – a strong post-war rallying to liberal values and to infusions of welfare state humaneness into society, and receiving from its poets a positive loyalty rarely seen during the previous decades of disillusion. (Though, of course, the attitude has had its complexities, which are very evident in Philip Larkin, our chief poet in this field.) Now a point I want to make is that this new positive loyalty is in some ways more restrictive on its poets than was the older pessimism. The liberal consciousness in its disillusions underlay not only the realist novel but much of romanticism, and in its crisis fathered the Modernist movement and sometimes dragged the entire cosmos into its disillusions. The new positive loyalty, whatever its complexities, cannot easily do this — Ted Hughes' attempt to drag a nightmarish dream-cosmos into the actualities of social inhumanity is hardly typical. What we typically tend to get is a form of realist poetry of fragmented insights, and a pushing of poetry into peripheral preoccupations — peripheral, that is, to the human mainstream. It was different in Pope's pre-Industrial Revolution day, when the positive loyalty could be, and was, central; not pushed to the periphery, as now. These remarks apply particularly, as I said, to post-war England. In America the unresolved dilemma of the age, 'the Tooth that nibbles at the soul' (no. 501) has perhaps been less effectively skimmed and filmed over (for it is in fact only a skimming and filming over that has taken place in English poetry; the real underlying issues, and their pressures, remain unexorcised and unresolved).

I think we can see Emily Dickinson's underlying consciousness in her poetry as primarily the liberal consciousness of her society in a crisis of awareness, but in her case controlled and understood in ways we have seen. This was the consciousness, and not any diminished or skimmed-over version of it, that she brought to her social realist insights in poetry; and it bred in the heart of her realism an acute, lyrically expressed, sense of loss of human value and potential — much of her finest poetry, including her love-poetry, is a realist-based lyricism of loss.

> The Sackcloth — hangs upon the nail —
> The Frock I used to wear —
> But where my moment of Brocade —
> My — drop — of India?
>
> (no. 430)

The realist insights underlying the lyricism of loss involved, as we have seen, an acute recognition of the reduction by the social order of the human person to a mere statistic ('mortal numeral') or to mere instrumentality in the service of things, the reduction of real human value to a meaninglessness given a cosmic extension in the lines:

> Our Periods may lie
> As Stars that drop anonymous
> From an abundant sky.
>
> (no. 999)

'Tis Units — make the Swarm' she reminds us in another poem, each unit a

'Being' of supreme real value. Here is the whole poem from which this line is taken:

> One Anguish – in a Crowd –
> A Minor thing – it sounds –
> And yet, unto the single Doe
> Attempted of the Hounds
>
> 'Tis Terror as consummate
> As Legions of Alarm
> Did leap, full flanked, upon the Host –
> 'Tis Units – make the Swarm –
>
> A Small Leech – on the Vitals –
> The sliver, in the Lung –
> The Bung out – of an Artery –
> Are scarce accounted – Harms –
>
> Yet mighty – by relation
> To that Repealless thing –
> A Being – impotent to end –
> When once it has begun –
>
> (no. 565)

Although the following poem has already been included in an earlier section, it seems necessary to repeat it here in the present context. The social realist insights are expressed in it with a clear understanding and completeness – it is remarkable how much is packed into its ten short lines:

> Bound – a trouble–
> And lives can bear it!
> Limit – how deep a bleeding go!
> So – many – drops – of vital scarlet –
> Deal with the soul
> As with Algebra!
>
> Tell it the Ages – to a cypher –
> And it will ache – contented – on –
> Sing – at its pain – as any Workman –
> Notching the fall of the Even Sun!
>
> (no. 269)

It will be useful and revealing to consider the above poem in conjunction with the following poem of the prison-house:

> A Prison gets to be a friend —
> Between its Ponderous face
> And Ours — a Kinsmanship express —
> And in its narrow Eyes —
>
> We come to look with gratitude
> For the appointed Beam
> It deal us — stated as our food —
> And hungered for — the same —
>
> We learn to know the Planks —
> That answer to Our feet —
> So miserable a sound — at first —
> Nor ever now — so sweet —
>
> As plashing in the Pools —
> When Memory was a Boy —
> But a Demurer Circuit —
> A Geometric Joy —
>
> The Posture of the Key
> That interrupt the Day
> To Our Endeavor — Not so real
> The Cheek of Liberty —
>
> As this Phantasm Steel —
> Whose features — Day and Night —
> Are present to us — as Our Own —
> And as escapeless — quite —
>
> The narrow Round — the Stint —
> The slow exchange of Hope —
> For something passiver — Content
> Too steep for looking up —
>
> The Liberty we knew
> Avoided — like a Dream
> Too wide for any Night but Heaven —
> If That — indeed — redeem —
>
> (no. 652)

Here, in this poem, is the modern human condition, the social condition, as Emily Dickinson sees it. Behind and immanent in the poem are the insights expressed in the previously quoted poem. The prison-house is not that of Lovelace's 'stone walls' and 'iron bars', not that of

> Bound – a trouble –
> And lives can bear it!

– but the world of 'Limit – how deep a bleeding go'. The 'shades of the prison-house' have grown darker and more intractable since Words-worth's day, in the transition from the world of the 'Immortality Ode' to that of *Little Dorritt*. What this poem conveys is the aching 'contented – on', the singing 'at its pain – as any Workman', of poem no. 269. Yet the mystifications and traditional consolations that make for the aching contented on ('Tell it the Ages – to a cypher') have for the poet become doubtful ('If That – indeed – redeem').

Now consider these lines:

> Not so real
> The Cheek of Liberty –
>
> As this Phantasm Steel –

We have seen something of Emily Dickinson's exploration of the existentialist response – the leap for liberty in face of the world of 'Manacle' or prison-house. Here, in these lines just quoted, we can perhaps read a failure of the existentialist response before the realist prison-scrutiny of the poem. Iris Murdoch[2] says of the existentialist impulse: 'An unexamined sense of the strength of the machine is combined with an illusion of leaping out of it'. If Emily Dickinson shared this illusion, in her realism she subjected it to a close critical scrutiny.

What these poems present is the imprisonment of real human value in the socio-economic necessities of the system.

> Limit – how deep a bleeding go!
> So – many – drops – of vital scarlet –
> Deal with the soul
> As with Algebra!

The 'So – many – drops – of vital scarlet' becomes a metaphor for the counting, statistical society which will 'Deal with the soul As with Algebra'. Yet, with the help of compensatory beliefs and hopes, the being enmeshed in these necessities will 'ache – contented – on – Sing – at its pain' and 'A Prison gets to be a friend'.

Here is another poem:

> From Blank to Blank –
> A Threadless Way
> I pushed Mechanic feet –
> To stop – or perish – or advance –
> Alike indifferent –
>
> If end I gained
> It ends beyond
> Indefinite disclosed –
> I shut my eyes – and groped as well
> 'Twas lighter – to be Blind –
>
> (no. 761)

Here again is 'The narrow Round – the Stint', the 'Circuit' and 'Geometric' movement of the prison-house poem, but expressed more bleakly and nakedly. Whatever the poet's intentions and the actual experience on which the poem was based, the significance of the poem as it stands extends beyond the purely personal and subjective into the consciousness of the age. As a picture of the effects on consciousness (so familiar in our time) of the reduction of work to the meaninglessness of mere instrumentality in the service of the socio-economic mechanics, whatever larger purpose of the system itself the work might serve, the poem could hardly be more precise and accurate –

> If end I gained
> It ends beyond
> Indefinite disclosed.

Consider now this poem:

> Not with a Club, the Heart is broken
> Nor with a Stone –
> A Whip so small you could not see it
> I've known
>
> To lash the Magic Creature
> Till it fell,

> Yet that Whip's Name
> Too noble then to tell.
>
> Magnanimous as Bird
> By Boy descried –
> Singing unto the Stone
> Of which it died –
>
> Shame need not crouch
> In such an Earth as Ours –
> Shame – stand erect –
> The Universe is yours.
>
> (no. 1304)

Just as it was not 'stone walls' or 'iron bars' that constituted the real prison of the human person, so in this poem it is not a 'Club' or 'Stone' that injures him. What is the 'Whip so small you could not see it' and whose name is 'Too noble . . . to tell'? That it was an inhumanity practised or sanctioned by society itself seems clear enough from the outburst in the final stanza –

> Shame need not crouch
> In such an Earth as Ours –
> Shame – stand erect –
> The Universe is yours.

It is an inhumanity in the human world, and not anything inherent in nature, that occasions such an outburst as this. Emily Dickinson's society provided examples of both slave labour and the free labour of the new emergent industrial order. The American Civil War took place during the period of her greatest creativity, and the iniquity of slave labour and the slave trade would have been readily apparent to her. But her perceptions seem to have penetrated beyond slave labour into the more difficult and problematical realm of free labour and the religious pressures associated with it. She seems to have been greatly struck by the apparent preparedness of people to accept and reconcile themselves to the conditions imposed on them – the third stanza of this poem recalls the 'ache – contented – on – ', the 'Sing – at its pain – as any Workman', of the 'Limit – how deep a bleeding' poem. But of course she is telling 'slant' the truth that she discerns, in accordance with her own precept:

> Tell all the Truth but tell it slant —
> Success in Circuit lies
> Too bright for our inform Delight
> The Truth's superb surprise
>
> As Lightning to the Children eased
> With explanation kind
> The Truth must dazzle gradually
> Or every man be blind —
>
> (no. 1129)

Another way of putting it is that truth must be presented not nakedly, but mediated in and through the complex of relationships of which it is the essence or organising principle. Properly mediated in this way, truth becomes not only truth but wisdom, a true wisdom which is not to be confused with the sort of wisdom that enables one to steer a safe passage away from awkward truths.

We have already noticed, in connection with the prison-house poem, the suggestion of a failure of the existentialist response — the leap for liberty in face of the world of manacle — before the realist prison-scrutiny of the poem. I want now to look a little further at this, the directing of the realism of the 'Solid Town' towards a realist self-scrutiny of her own responses to the situation as she saw it.

Here, for example, is another poem which subjects an existentialist impulse, or one akin to it, to a realist self-scrutiny:

> Of Bronze — and Blaze —
> The North — Tonight —
> So adequate — it forms —
> So preconcerted with itself —
> So distant — to alarms —
> An Unconcern so sovereign
> To Universe, or me —
> Infects my simple spirit
> With Taints of Majesty —
> Till I take vaster attitudes —
> And strut upon my stem —
> Disdaining Men, and Oxygen,
> For Arrogance of them —
>
> My Splendors, are Menagerie —
> But their Competeless Show

> Will entertain the Centuries
> When I, am long ago,
> An Island in dishonored Grass —
> Whom none but Beetles — know.
>
> (no. 290)

It is the sublime spectacle of the Northern Lights that has caused this infection of the spirit with 'Taints of Majesty'. Iris Murdoch,[3] speaking of Kant's view of the sublime, says: 'The spectacle of huge and appalling things can indeed exhilarate, but usually in a way that is less than excellent. Much existentialist thought relies upon such a "thinking reed" reaction which is nothing more than a form of romantic self-assertion.' And again: 'We experience the Sublime when we confront the awful contingency of nature or of human fate and return into ourselves with a proud shudder of rational power.' Emily Dickinson's poem portrays precisely this situation and this judgment on it, with remarkable precision and understanding.

Here is another poem:

> So large my Will
> The little that I may
> Embarrasses
> Like gentle infamy —
>
> Affront to Him
> For whom the Whole were small
> Affront to me
> Who know His Meed of all.
>
> Earth at the best
> Is but a scanty Toy —
> Bought, carried Home
> To Immortality
>
> It looks so small
> We chiefly wonder then
> At our Conceit
> In purchasing.
>
> (no. 1024)

This poem, from its viewpoint in old tradition, makes its own gentle appraisal of the validity or the scope of the existentialist will. The poem reads like a putting to rest of the restless existentialist impulse in her deeper vision of the real. It is another poem of the innocence of the real, making the real of old tradition live again and assert its human meaning and value through all the questionings of our time. We must distinguish between the perennial human real and the specific realities of our own historical order with which this section has been largely concerned, reserving for each its proper place in our understanding, the former serving as the latter's necessary ground of being.

NOTES

1. See, for example, A. Alvarez's Introduction to his selection, *The New Poetry* (Harmondsworth: Penguin, 1962). He speaks of what he calls 'the gentility principle' and a 'relative failure of talent' in the English poetry of the period. See also Donald Davie's *Thomas Hardy and British Poetry*.
2. Iris Murdoch, *The Sovereignty of Good*, p. 48.
3. Ibid., pp. 73 and 81–2.

8

The Realism of Love and Death

I

In this sub-section I want to look briefly at some of Emily Dickinson's love-poetry. Consider first this poem:

> I had not minded – Walls –
> Were Universe – one Rock –
> And far I heard his silver Call
> The other side the Block –
>
> I'd tunnel – till my Groove
> Pushed sudden thro' to his –
> Then my face take her Recompense –
> The looking in his Eyes –
>
> But 'tis a single Hair –
> A filament – a law –
> A Cobweb – wove in Adamant –
> A Battlement – of Straw –
>
> A limit like the Veil
> Unto the Lady's face –
> But every Mesh – a Citadel –
> And Dragons – in the Crease
>
> (no. 398)

Once again, it is not Lovelace's 'stone walls' and 'iron bars', but the adamantine intangibles of the prison-house that Emily Dickinson discerned. 'A great prince in prison lies'. But love is the victim not only of social obstructions, but of inhibitions in its own psychology, and sometimes and most powerfully, as we shall see, of the commands of a deeper reality; and all of these enter into the making of love's prison-house.

Emily Dickinson's love-poetry is typically a realist-based lyricism of the loss or renunciation of love. It must be understood, however, that it is not the familiar stereotype of the world with its conventional relationships and rewards well lost for love or prevailing against the demands of love. Emily Dickinson ends one of her poems with these two stanzas:

> The Vision — pondered long —
> So plausible becomes
> That I esteem the fiction — real —
> The Real — fictitious seems —
>
> How bountiful the Dream —
> What Plenty — it would be —
> Had all my Life but been Mistake
> Just rectified — in Thee.
>   (no. 646)

The judgement expressed in these two stanzas is far removed from the stereotype referred to above. Reality is in the poet's discernments of the real; it is not the conventional world's but the poet's imperative, and therefore in the end inescapable.

> I envy Seas, whereon He rides —
> I envy Spokes of Wheels
> Of Chariots, that Him convey —
> I envy Crooked Hills
>
> That gaze upon His Journey —
> How easy All can see
> What is forbidden utterly
> As Heaven — unto me!
>
> I envy Nests of Sparrows —
> That dot His distant Eaves —
> The wealthy Fly, upon His Pane —
> The happy — happy Leaves —
>
> That just abroad His Window
> Have Summer's leave to play —
> The Ear Rings of Pizarro
> Could not obtain for me —

I envy Light – that wakes Him –
And Bells – that boldly ring
To tell Him it is Noon, abroad –
Myself – be Noon to Him –

Yet interdict – my Blossom –
And abrogate – my Bee –
Lest Noon in Everlasting Night –
Drop Gabriel – and Me –

                              (no. 498)

The command of the poet's own reality rings out unmistakably in the final stanza of the poem. It is in the very language of the command, in the interdiction and the abrogation. There is a Shakespearean splendour in the passage.

T. S. Eliot once described the lyric as the voice of the poet talking to himself. Such a lyric is very clearly the following poem:

It might be lonelier
Without the Loneliness –
I'm so accustomed to my Fate –
Perhaps the Other – Peace –

Would interrupt the Dark –
And crowd the little Room –
Too scant – by Cubits – to contain
The Sacrament – of Him –

I am not used to Hope –
It might intrude upon –
Its sweet parade – blaspheme the place –
Ordained to Suffering –

It might be easier
To fail – with Land in Sight –
Than gain – My Blue Peninsula –
To perish – of Delight –

                              (no. 405)

In this next poem reality's questioning of love is carried beyond the grave:

I cannot live with You –
It would be Life –
And Life is over there –
Behind the Shelf

The Sexton keeps the Key to –
Putting up
Our Life – His Porcelain –
Like a Cup –

Discarded of the Housewife –
Quaint – or Broke –
A newer Sevres pleases –
Old Ones crack –

I could not die – with You –
For One must wait
To shut the Other's Gaze down –
You – could not –

And I – Could I stand by
And see You – freeze –
Without my Right of Frost –
Death's privilege?

Nor could I rise – with You –
Because Your Face
Would put out Jesus' –
That New Grace

Glow plain – and foreign
On my homesick Eye –
Except that You than He
Shone closer by –

They'd judge Us – How –
For You – served Heaven – You know,
Or sought to –
I could not –

Because You saturated Sight –
And I had no more Eyes

For sordid excellence
As Paradise

And were You lost, I would be –
Though My Name
Rang loudest
On the Heavenly fame –

And were You – saved –
And I – condemned to be
Where You were not –
That self – were Hell to Me –

So We must meet apart –
You there – I – here –
With just the Door ajar
That Oceans are – and Prayer –
And that White Sustenance –
Despair –

(no. 640)

Not only earthly love, but the romantic dream of love in death and after death, eternal love, are subjected to the realist scrutiny. Earthly love continued into Heaven would diminish or distort the realities of Heaven too. The last six lines are a supreme moment in the lyricism of loss.

Here is a little poem which I think can appropriately follow those six lines:

So set its Sun in Thee
What Day be dark to me –
What Distance – far –
So I the Ships may see
That touch – how seldomly –
Thy Shore?

(no. 808)

The despair in the brave assertions of this poem ('that White Sustenance – Despair –') enforces, and finds expression in, the modulation of the grammar into the subjunctive.

Here is another poem of the realist-based lyricism of loss – the controlling realism of the piece is firmly present in the second stanza, in the reappraisal of the drought and dew of subjective feeling through the image of the Caspian sands and sea:

> To lose thee — sweeter than to gain
> All other hearts I knew.
> 'Tis true the drought is destitute,
> But then, I had the dew!
>
> The Caspian has its realms of sand,
> Its other realm of sea.
> Without the sterile perquisite,
> No Caspian could be.
>
> (no. 1754)

This little group of love-poems must necessarily end with the following poem — it is one of the greatest love-poems ever written, a fusion of love, death, heaven and hell to reveal an abiding reality of human experience at its intensest and profoundest:

> My life closed twice before its close —
> It yet remains to see
> If Immortality unveil
> A third event to me
>
> So huge, so hopeless to conceive
> As these that twice befell.
> Parting is all we know of heaven,
> And all we need of hell.
>
> (no. 1732)

II

As a prelude to what follows in this sub-section, I want to include the following little poem of Emily Dickinson's:

> Some we see no more, Tenements of Wonder
> Occupy to us though perhaps to them
> Simpler are the Days than the Supposition
> Their removing Manners
> Leave us to presume

> That oblique Belief which we call Conjecture
> Grapples with a Theme stubborn as Sublime
> Able as the Dust to equip its feature
> Adequate as Drums
> To enlist the Tomb.
>
> (no. 1221)

Tradition has an abundant repertoire of consolatory beliefs, rituals, periphrastic phrases and so on, to remove the sting from the inescapable reality of death, to deflect or insulate the consciousness from a naked confrontation with the naked unspeakable. The contemplation of the grave also seems to lend itself to a sort of quaint fantasising – for example, Housman's fantasised version ('The night is freezing fast') of Wordsworth's noble 'A slumber did my spirit seal' – which I suppose is another way of not confronting the naked reality – this fantasised death is warm with wooden overcoats and suchlike wrappings. Emily Dickinson is not immune from this fantasising tendency; her interest in the subject of death coupled with her inventive powers in poetry must have made it a sore temptation for her. Her major death-themes, however, are in a different category. We have seen something of these themes in previous sections, the death–time linkage and the special significance of death in the existentialist scheme. To conclude this section on the realist poet, I want to look briefly at the realism of death through her eyes.

> I felt a Funeral, in my Brain,
> And Mourners to and fro
> Kept treading – treading – till it seemed
> That Sense was breaking through –
>
> And when they all were seated,
> A Service, like a Drum –
> Kept beating – beating – till I thought
> My Mind was going numb –
>
> And then I heard them lift a Box
> And creak across my Soul
> With those same Boots of Lead, again,
> Then Space – began to toll,
>
> As all the Heavens were a Bell,
> And Being, but an Ear,

> And I, and Silence, some strange Race
> Wrecked, solitary, here —
>
> And then a Plank in Reason, broke,
> And I dropped down, and down —
> And hit a World, at every plunge,
> And Finished knowing — then —
>
> (no. 280)

To follow this remarkably successful attempt to penetrate through the ritual of burial to the reality of death as a lived experience, here is a poem of the observed face of death, but observed with a strict, unflinching realism:

> 'Twas warm — at first — like Us —
> Until there crept upon
> A Chill — like frost upon a Glass —
> Till all the scene — be gone.
>
> The Forehead copied Stone —
> The Fingers grew too cold
> To ache — and like a Skater's Brook —
> The busy eyes — congealed —
>
> It straightened — that was all —
> It crowded Cold to Cold —
> It multiplied indifference —
> As Pride were all it could —
>
> And even when with Cords —
> 'Twas lowered, like a Weight —
> It made no Signal, nor demurred,
> But dropped like Adamant.
>
> (no. 519)

In another poem Emily Dickinson speaks of 'Death's Ethereal Scorn', just as in this poem 'It multiplied indifference — As Pride were all it could'.
Here is another poem:

> How many times these low feet staggered —
> Only the soldered mouth can tell —

Try – can you stir the awful rivet –
Try – can you lift the hasps of steel!

Stroke the cool forehead – hot so often –
Lift – if you care – the listless hair –
Handle the adamantine fingers
Never a thimble – more – shall wear –

Buzz the dull flies – on the chamber window –
Brave – shines the sun through the freckled pane –
Fearless – the cobweb swings from the ceiling –
Indolent Housewife – in Daisies – lain!

(no. 187)

Emily Dickinson says elsewhere, 'The Truth, is Bald, and Cold' (no. 281). But if, in immediate and direct confrontation with death, 'The Truth, is Bald, and Cold', a true realism recognises death not just in isolation but in all its human contexts, integral with the processes of living and the whole pattern of life; recognises, for example, in these contexts, the reality of human courage and dignity in unflinching confrontation with death.

No Notice gave She, but a Change –
No Message, but a Sigh –
For Whom, the Time did not suffice
That She should specify.

She was not warm, though Summer shone
Nor scrupulous of cold
Though Rime by Rime, the steady Frost
Upon Her Bosom piled –

Of shrinking ways – she did not fright
Though all the Village looked –
But held Her gravity aloft –
And met the gaze – direct –

And when adjusted like a Seed
In careful fitted Ground
Unto the Everlasting Spring
And hindered but a Mound

Her Warm return, if so she chose –
And We, imploring drew –
Removed our invitation by
As Some She never knew –

(no. 804)

The simple human dignity in this poem, in its confrontation with approaching death, is well within the jurisdiction of the real.

Nor do I think that the following poem, and the sentiments expressed in it, can be faulted from the standpoint of a true realism of death in its living contexts:

We Cover Thee – Sweet Face –
Not that We tire of Thee –
But that Thyself fatigue of Us –
Remember – as Thou go –
We follow Thee until
Thou notice Us – no more –
And then – reluctant – turn away
To Con Thee o'er and o'er –

And blame the scanty love
We were Content to show –
Augmented – Sweet – a Hundred fold –
If Thou would'st take it – now –

(no. 482)

To conclude this group of death-poems, here are three poems which differ from others in relating more to the tomb itself than to the dead or dying person.

First, this:

Not any sunny tone
From any fervent zone
Find entrance there –
Better a grave of Balm
Toward human nature's home –
And Robins near –
Than a stupendous Tomb
Proclaiming to the Gloom
How dead we are –

(no. 1674)

This next poem could perhaps serve as an epitaph on a tomb in appropriate circumstances:

> Left in immortal Youth
> On that low Plain
> That hath nor Retrospection
> Nor Again –
> Ransomed from years –
> Sequestered from Decay
> Canceled like Dawn
> In comprehensive Day –
>> (no. 1289)

Finally, this poem:

> After a hundred years
> Nobody knows the Place
> Agony that enacted there
> Motionless as Peace
>
> Weeds triumphant ranged
> Strangers strolled and spelled
> At the lone Orthography
> Of the Elder Dead
>
> Winds of Summer Fields
> Recollect the way –
> Instinct picking up the Key
> Dropped by memory –
>> (no. 1147)

9

The Garment of Surprise

Mr Earnshaw once bought a couple of colts at the parish fair, and gave the lads each one. Heathcliff took the handsomest, but it soon fell lame, and when he discovered it, he said to Hindley –
'You must exchange horses with me.' . . . [He] went on with his intention; exchanging saddles and all.

Doubtless Catherine marked the difference between her friends, as one came in and the other went out. The contrast resembled what you see in exchanging a bleak, hilly, coal country for a beautiful fertile valley.

These two quotations are from Chapters 4 and 8 respectively of *Wuthering Heights*.
Emily Dickinson, in the last stanza of one of her poems, speaks of

> A quality of loss
> Affecting our Content
> As Trade had suddenly encroached
> Upon a Sacrament.
> (no. 812)

These lines can be compared to Emily Brontë's image of the bleak coal country and the beautiful fertile valley. Yet there are differences. Emily Brontë's vision includes an intimation of a new usurping human order (the exchange of horses and saddles) encroaching upon an older human order and bringing with it both a change of consciousness in people and a change in the aspect nature wears to that consciousness. Emily Dickinson's image, however, springs from the withdrawal from the landscape of a special early spring light, leaving the light of common day in which trade and its encroachments on qualitative nature is a given fact of the ordinary consciousness. Emily Dickinson's vision in this respect is two-dimensional, where Emily Brontë's is three-dimensional. For Emily

Dickinson the world of trade is the actual of everyday life, the contingent masquerading as the real, capable only of quantitative change, over-spreading and obscuring the underlying qualitative real; but changing light can bring about a qualitative change in the consciousness and in nature's aspect. Her light is not just the ordinary transforming light of common experience, but is also a transcendental shining, like Words-worth's light penetrating and counteracting the 'shades of the prison-house' in the 'Immortality Ode'. To take another example from Emily Dickinson of the changing light with its transcendental overtones, here is a poem of the 'Act of evening' on the landscape:

> The Mountains stood in Haze –
> The Valleys stopped below
> And went or waited as they liked
> The River and the Sky.
>
> At leisure was the Sun –
> His interests of Fire
> A little from remark withdrawn –
> The Twilight spoke the Spire,
>
> So soft upon the Scene
> The Act of evening fell
> We felt how neighborly a Thing
> Was the Invisible.
>
> (no. 1278)

In *Wuthering Heights*, however, the light breaking out towards the end of the work is not primarily this transcendental light, but springs from the liberation of Heathcliff's prison-house in the emergence of a new human order (and even Heathcliff's own assumption of the reins and saddles, with all its negative aspects, had marked an advance on an old order that had grown effete). This sense of history as a living qualitative process of human growth and value in the midst of and transcending vicissitudes is, as we have seen, foreign to Emily Dickinson's vision, the prison-house of her consciousness presenting itself in the guise of a natural necessity regardless of the underlying pressures of history on it, and to which she must make her own responses of the kinds we have seen; and in this she is truly representative of the consciousness of the age – even her poem in praise of the radical heroes (no. 295, included in Chapter 4) is a celebration of human grandeur in inevitable defeat, in the authentic existentialist modes. Time as a qualitative flowing is stopped in the time of clock, calendar and the celestial mechanics, the time of

> Slow tramp the Centuries,
> And the Cycles wheel.
> (no. 160)

When the light breaks, it comes, as in the two poems quoted above, from sources above and outside history. It can illumine, but not change, the temporal order, though it can change the individual consciousness and the aspect nature wears to that consciousness; it can, in fact, increase the sense of desolation:

> Had I not seen the Sun
> I could have borne the shade
> But Light a newer Wilderness
> My Wilderness has made —
> (no. 1233)

This is her short answer, and the age's answer, to the Wordsworthian optimism of the light seen from amidst the prison shades. The ultimate optimism of *Wuthering Heights* is of another kind.

At this point, I think, Shakespeare can be our best guide — in particular, the Shakespeare of *King Lear*, the supreme work of our era, written in the era's dawn, in the transition from the old order to the new, in the early years of the seventeenth century.[1]

Shakespeare, probing into realities of historic change in his day, came face to face with Goneril and Edmund. Emily Brontë confronted Heathcliff who resembled 'a bleak, hilly, coal country' and had his own ways of effecting the exchange of horses and saddles. If we wish to find a Shakespearean pattern for the ultimate optimism of *Wuthering Heights*, however, it is not to *King Lear*, but pre-eminently to *Macbeth* that we must turn — to the advancing green branches and the prospect of restoring the broken harmonies of nature, man and society in the emergence of a new regime. In *King Lear*, despite a prospect of better things after the downfall of Goneril and Edmund, in the end 'all's cheerless, dark and deadly' in the ultimate cosmos-questioning tragedy of the drama. Dr Johnson, in the relative optimism of the Augustan phase of our era, found the ultimate tragedy of *King Lear* intolerable, a relapse from the social or divine justice of Goneril's and Edmund's downfall into sheer meaninglessness. Perhaps we are better placed now to understand the depth and penetration of Shakespeare's insight at the dawn of a brilliant but complex era. I have tried to show how Emily Dickinson, who in a major part of her work is essentially a poet of the cosmos-questioning tragic vision, can be an aid to the understanding.

Earlier, in *King John*, Shakespeare had said:

> The life, the right and truth of all this realm
> Is fled to heaven; and England now is left
> To tug and scamble and to part by the teeth
> The unowned interest of proud-swelling state.

But the point of the cosmos-questioning element in *King Lear* and in Emily Dickinson is that it is a questioning of whether 'the life, the right and truth' can be found even in heaven ('As flies to wanton boys are we to the gods', or Emily Dickinson's Newtonian God pursuing his 'Perturbless Plan' regardless) – the prime source of the cosmic doubt is in the changed attitude to, and aspect of, nature expressed in Edmund's soliloquy 'Thou, nature, art my goddess'. It is when these values are lost even in heaven, leaving nothing but the 'tug and scamble' of the temporal order as sanctioned by the new view of nature, that 'all's cheerless, dark and deadly', eclipsing utterly the final optimism of *Macbeth*. In her poem 'It was not Death' (no. 510), Emily Dickinson seems to be looking straight into the 'cheerless, dark and deadly' of *King Lear*:

> And 'twas like Midnight, some –
>
> When everything that ticked – has stopped –
> And Space stares all around –
> Or Grisly frosts – first Autumn morns,
> Repeal the Beating Ground –
>
> But, most, like Chaos – Stopless – cool –
> Without a Chance, or Spar –
> Or even a Report of Land –
> To justify – Despair.

Still using Shakespeare as a guide, I want to turn now to another of his themes – to his recognition, in *The Winter's Tale*, of the primacy of 'great creating nature', his implicit presentation of nature, with its stabilities and cyclical recurrences, as man's ground of being and ultimate security amidst the vicissitudes and accidents and human pretensions of social life and history.

Here is a little poem of Emily Dickinson's:

> A little Madness in the Spring
> Is wholesome even for the King,
> But God be with the Clown —
> Who ponders this tremendous scene —
> This whole Experiment of Green —
> As if it were his own!
>
> (no. 1333)

'Great creating nature', 'This whole Experiment of Green' — this little song might have come straight out of the world of *The Winter's Tale*, and perhaps it did — she knew Shakespeare well, and has her own short lyric versions of Shakespeare's counterpoising or underpinning of the 'cheerless, dark and deadly' with the central theme of *The Winter's Tale*. Even if the celestial mechanics are all of heaven we know, at least their mathematical certainties are the source and guarantee of the life-sustaining certainties and stabilities of nature:

> Trusty as the stars
> Who quit their shining working
> Prompt as when I lit them
> In Genesis' new house,
> Durable as dawn
> Whose antiquated blossom
> Makes a world's suspense
> Perish and rejoice.
>
> (no. 1369)

We might almost, in this little poem, be present at the making of the world by absolute decree (or from cosmic necessity) — a world suspended in the timeless time and ticking to the recurring time of the celestial systems, of which it is of course a member. But for nature to be 'great creating nature', engaged in its 'Experiment of Green', time in its other aspect as a qualitative flowing, with its leaps from quantitative change into qualitative newness and renewal, must manifest itself in and through the chemical and living process. It is this, the qualitative flowing, that gives nature, in Emily Dickinson's words, its 'Garment of Surprise', its inexhaustible depths and riches and capacity to surprise, if we can see beyond the stereotypes of everyday.

It is characteristic of the qualitative process that it leaps from one level to a higher level; leaps, for example, across the discontinuous continuity between unconscious nature and the human – though of course the process is complex and uneven, and far from being an unbroken advance to higher things.

Here is a poem by Emily Dickinson of the pattern and process of qualitative change in the human individual consciousness (the characteristic and necessary relation of pattern to process is vividly and accurately revealed in the metaphorical pattern of the event as presented in the poem):

> My Cocoon tightens – Colors tease –
> I'm feeling for the Air –
> A dim capacity for Wings
> Demeans the Dress I wear –
>
> A power of Butterfly must be –
> The Aptitude to fly
> Meadows of Majesty implies
> And easy Sweeps of Sky –
>
> So I must baffle at the Hint
> And cipher at the Sign
> And make much blunder, if at last
> I take the clue divine –
>
> (no. 1099)

Both Milton and Dante used the image of wings to symbolise a qualitative change to a new level in the human consciousness. In *Paradise Lost* the new-fallen Adam and Even

> fancy that they feel
> Divinity within them breeding wings
> Wherewith to scorn the Earth.

Emily Dickinson is well aware that the promise of new strengths and freedoms in qualitative growth of this kind in the human consciousness can infect the spirit, in her own words, 'With Taints of Majesty'. In the last stanza of her poem she seems to be recognising and guarding against the danger; the stanza is all uncertainty and implied warning – 'baffling' and 'ciphering', making 'much blunder', 'if I take' (not 'when I take'). Here, at the end of the wings passage at the close of Canto 27 of the *Purgatorio*, are Virgil's parting words to Dante:[2]

No more expect my word, nor my sign. Free, upright, and whole, is thy
will, and 'twere a fault not to act according to its prompting; wherefore
I do crown and mitre these over thyself.

Thus the wings of qualitative newness appear at both the beginning and
the end of the human pilgrimage within the Christian scheme. At what
'odd Fork' along the way the experience expressed in Emily Dickinson's
poem is to be located, she does not specify. Her poem is an imaginative
presentation of the essence of the pattern of the event itself, and can thus
exercise its potency in whatever appropriate contexts we imaginatively
put it – this is how the creative imagination can work, and why
Shakespeare is always stirring up new meanings to the imagination; the
creative imagination itself has its being in and is a living part of the whole
qualitative process in all its complex interrelationships and with its
'Garment of Surprise', but operating at the human level.

In the human sphere, the process of qualitative change can sometimes
be a shattering experience, especially if the initial build-up of pressures
encounters strong resistance from the existing order. Consider this poem
of Emily Dickinson's:

> He fumbles at your Soul
> As Players at the Keys
> Before they drop full Music on –
> He stuns you by degrees –
> Prepares your brittle Nature
> For the Ethereal Blow
> By fainter Hammers – further heard –
> Then nearer – Then so slow
> Your Breath has time to straighten –
> Your Brain – to bubble Cool –
> Deals – One – imperial – Thunderbolt –
> That scalps your naked Soul –
>
> When Winds take Forests in their Paws –
>
> The Universe – is still –
>
> (no. 315)

We have only to transfer in imagination this poem from its setting in the
individual consciousness to a wider context of human affairs, to see that it
also expresses the very pattern of a process of decisive historic change –

the imagery itself is very appropriate to this.

I must return briefly to the central theme of *The Winter's Tale*. Consider these lines from Act IV, Scene iv:

> Nature is made better by no mean,
> But nature makes that mean: so, over that art
> Which you say adds to nature, is an art
> That nature makes. You see, sweet maid, we marry
> A gentler scion to the wildest stock,
> And make conceive a bark of baser kind
> By bud of nobler race: this is an art
> Which does mend nature, change it rather, but
> The art itself is nature.

The primacy of 'great creating nature' — but man participates in the creative work as nature's instrument and art to raise nature to new levels. (This is the very opposite to using his powers to impose his will on nature for his own separate ends.) Though of course the relationship is necessarily a complex one; for man is not only part of, but also something apart from nature. It is in the realm of history that he lives his apartness from nature. Yet he is still a part of nature, not in spite of but in and through his apartness; and it is in history — in the history that, beyond mere contingency and crime, is a qualitative process of human growth and value — that he tries to re-establish on new levels his and his society's broken harmonies with nature; and it is here that the true human dimension is to be found. Of course, it has not been, and will not be, all sweetness and light. The distortions of man in history are immense. Yet it is only here, in and through the historic process, that he will recover on new levels his true creative place in nature. The struggle has still very far to go.

However, I should like Emily Dickinson to have the last word in this study:

> In snow thou comest —
> Thou shalt go with the resuming ground,
> The sweet derision of the crow,
> And Glee's advancing sound.
>
> In fear thou comest —
> Thou shalt go at such a gait of joy

That man anew embark to live
Upon the depth of thee.

(no. 1669)

NOTES

1. See the study of *King Lear* by John F. Danby, *Shakespeare's Doctrine of Nature* (London: Faber & Faber, 1948).
2. In the prose translation from Dent's Temple Classics edition.

Index

First lines of Emily Dickinson's poems are printed in *italic*.